ANDREA MARTIN'S
LADY PARTS

HarperCollins*Publishers*

HarperCollins books may be purchased for educational, business,
or sales promotional use through our Special Markets Department.

HarperCollins Publishers Ltd
2 Bloor Street East, 20th Floor
Toronto, Ontario, Canada
M4W 1A8

www.harpercollins.ca

Library and Archives Canada Cataloguing in Publication
information is available upon request.

ISBN 9780062387288

Printed and bound in the United States of America
RRD 9 8 7 6 5 4 3 2 1

ANDREA MARTIN'S
LADY PARTS

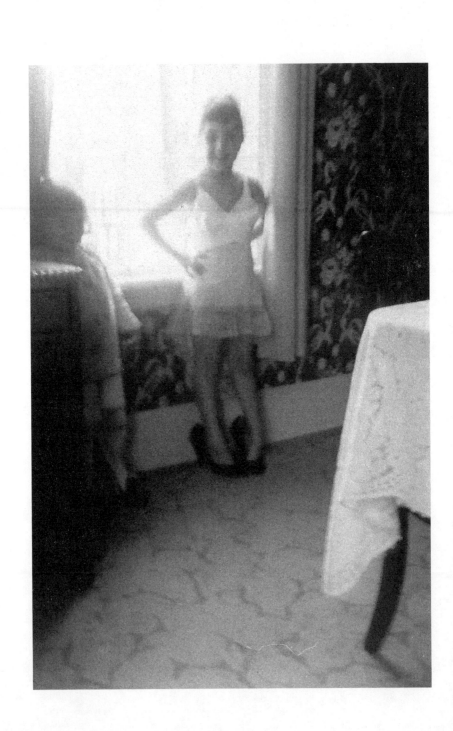

To Canada, where it all began.
My marriage.
My children.
My career.
Justin Bieber.

Contents

Introduction

Hello, everyone. And welcome. Before you begin reading my book, I need to come clean and set the record straight. I am not Canadian. I'm American. *Gasp.* I know, I've disappointed you, maybe even angered you. If you want to return this book and get a refund, I don't blame you. Who wants to invest time in a liar? How can you trust me now, or for that matter, anything I say in this book? Even Oprah wouldn't have me on her network.

Please, before you judge me too harshly, I need you to know I never meant any harm. Greater powers than I have spun my tale of mistaken identity out of control over the years, until it's become fact. You, Canada, have always been kind and warm and welcoming to me. You've opened your hearts and pocketbooks. You have made me one of your own. And now I spit in your face. I disgust myself.

What is the origin of my deceit?

My assimilation into Canadian life was not any elaborate scheme to use or exploit the good people of Canada. I did not come to Canada to dodge the draft. It was neither a court order, nor a kidnapping nor witness protection that brought me to your fine country. The fact is, I visited Toronto in 1970, fell in love with the city on the first day, and stayed. From that moment on, I was an honorary Canadian, and no one ever asked to see my papers. Well, airport security did, not to mention Canadian immigration, the IRS, and the border patrol, but you lovely people with television sets did not. And so the myth continued.

For the last forty years, I've called Canada my home, or my second home, but out of all my homes, Canada has been my favourite. Okay, now I'm pandering.

If you stick with me past this disclaimer, I promise I won't disappoint you. I'll fill you in on the details of my life, all the juicy, indulgent, humiliating details of my dual existence and how I've come to be known (in my inflated head) as Canada's favourite illegitimate child.

Part One

Part One

Perky Tits

W hen Steve Martin suggests a title for your book, you listen.

At first, upon hearing the title, I felt uncomfortable, and a little embarrassed. I was one of eight dinner guests at Steve's home, and we were all sitting around the table, where an animated conversation about my forthcoming book was as delicious to my ears as his chef's choice of arctic char and aged New York steak was to my palate.

"*Perky Tits!*" Steve Martin yelled out. "That should be the title of your book." The seven other dinner guests— Marty Short; Eugene Levy and his wife, Deb Divine; Laurie MacDonald and her husband, Walter Parkes; a couple I was meeting for the first time, the distinguished author Frederick Tuten and his partner, Karen Marta, an editor for *Vogue*—all of them began to laugh. Happy for the attention but nevertheless shocked by the description of my private parts, I was intrigued as to why Steve had come up with *that* title.

"Wow, what made you think of that, Steve?" I asked, giggling and flattered that he even cared I was writing a book. How could I question the great Steve Martin, whose best-selling books and their titles *Shopgirl*, *Cruel Shoes*, and *Born Standing Up* are genius? But aren't all those titles much tamer than *Perky Tits*? Was he being facetious? Was he just tossing out a funny title to get a laugh?

Believe me, I was grateful and relieved that someone else was suggesting a possible title for my book. I had been fixating on titles for months. It was a fabulous trick I had unconsciously discovered as I convinced myself I was writing my book, when all along I was just procrastinating my perky tits off. Steve and I began to engage in book-title banter, and the rest of the dinner guests weighed in. I threw out a couple of my ideas.

"*She's the Best Thing in It.*"

Silence, mixed with disdain.

"*TMI: Too Much Information.*"

"Dated," Steve said.

I offered up another. "*You Look Like Someone.*"

"Too self-deprecating!" someone else yelled out.

"How about *Fake Beaver*?" I asked timidly as I began to lose my bravura and settle into my comfort zone of low self-esteem. "I think it's good because it describes my fake status in Canada as a Canadian, when all along I am an American, with immigration status, living in Canada, which is home to the beaver . . ." Oh boy, what the hell was I talking about? I started back-pedalling.

"No, too vulgar," someone said. "*Perky Tits* is much better."

"Yes, yes," another voice chimed in, "*Perky Tits*. I would buy that book. *Perky Tits*. It describes your personality. *Perky Tits*. It cuts right through. There's Tina Fey's *Bossypants*, and Andrea Martin's *Perky Tits*."

"Really?" I said weakly, slowly doubting myself. It was clear I was an uninspired fraud, not an author. I had no pulse on what would sell. On who I was. I was definitely going to give my advance back to HarperCollins.

"It's a part of your past," Steve said. "It's relevant."

How did he know my perky tits were a part of my past? I guess he'd read Paul Shaffer's autobiography, in which one chapter is dedicated to my pert boobies. He would have read that, when I was younger, I wasn't shy about saying the word "tits," nor, for that matter, showing them to anyone who was mildly interested. In fact, the chapter in Paul's book is entitled "You've Seen These Haven't You?" Yes, it is true, during the '70s when I first met Paul and we were both starting out in our careers, I was a freewheeling breast exposer. I must have been fond of my boobies, because I remember flashing them more often than not. But didn't everyone do stuff like that then? And why recall those boob-flashing moments in my life and name a book after them?

Why did "perky tits" have such negative implications for me, and why was I being so resistant to a title that everyone at the dinner table said would propel them to buy the book?

"Perky." I had always hated that word, a word too often used to describe my persona. Is that the only way I came across, cheerful and lively? What was I, a Jack Russell? Where were the other adjectives used to describe the real me: dark, deep, enigmatic, profound, complex, loyal, intelligent? I'm a Doberman pinscher, goddamnit. I have Doberman pinscher written all over me. "Perky" was synonymous with superficial. "Vanessa Redgrave is mesmerizing and heartbreaking as Mary Tyrone, in *Long Day's Journey into Night*, and Andrea Martin as her maid, Bea, is perky." That's the kind of review I was used to. Not that there's a maid called Bea in *Long Day's Journey*, but if there were one and I had been cast in the part, you can bet your perky tits that I would have been called "perky."

Years ago, at the height of *SCTV*, a journalist from *Playboy* wrote an article on the seven cast members. He described his first impression of each of us. Catherine O'Hara was enigmatic. John Candy, warm, inclusive. Andrea Martin, he wrote, was perky and accommodating. There is only one word, in my opinion, worse than "perky" and it's "accommodating." Who'd want to be around that person all the time? Well, me, if she were my maid.

Here's the thing about writing a book about yourself. You hope you'll do a good job about revealing who you really are, or what's the purpose of writing? Sure, I hope you're entertained, and that you get a couple of good laughs out of this book, but in the end, I'd like you to know that there's more to me than just being perky, which doesn't mean that I won't use the title Steve Martin suggested. I don't want to hurt his feelings. After all, I'm accommodating . . .

Wait, wait. I have it!

Complex Tits, by Andrea Martin. It has *New York Times* bestselling book written all over it.

Nota bene:

In the end, my beloved editor nixed the title *Perky Tits*. He was concerned that people would be offended by the word "perky."

It's My Roots, Johnny

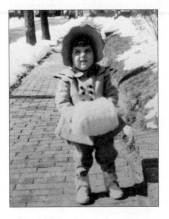

I was born in Portland, Maine, in 1947, and although Maine is one of thirteen states in America that border Canada, this fact is meaningless to my story. However, it *is* interesting if you're a geography buff. Thirteen states? That's surprising, isn't it? Didn't you think it was more like eight?

Anyway, I have always thought that I was born in the wrong place, at the wrong time. I should have been born in the '20s. I'm more of a flapper kind of gal. Think Zelda Fitzgerald, but not as heavily medicated. Big eyes, curly brown hair, able to do the Charleston really well. Here are some other adjectives people have used to describe me: perky (again!), quirky, loud, and fun. (Also: over the top, not subtle, too broad, give someone else a chance, pulling focus, chewing the scenery, and rat-like.)

I'm Armenian. My grandfather's name was Papazian. He came to Maine in 1920 and saw the name "Martin" on the side of a truck. So he took the name. He also took the truck. You know who else is Armenian? The Kardashian sisters. In fact, they have brought so much positive energy to the country that Armenia is thinking of changing its national anthem to "I Like Big Butts and I Cannot Lie."

In any case, I grew up in Maine, home to Republican country clubbers, yachts, and lobsters, about as far away from my reality then as a penis is to my reality today. I was proud to say I was from Maine, though. I still am. It has an exotic feel to it, especially if you're an actress. With the exception of Linda Lavin and the twenty-something, multi-talented Oscar-nominee Anna Kendrick, how many actresses do you know who hail from Maine? Well, Bette Davis used to have a home there, and her then husband Gary Merrill often frequented bars wearing skirts. But they were anomalies. They were transplanted movie stars. I was an authentic Mainiac, so I could claim the title Actress Born in Maine. Pine trees, the ocean, and fried clams were in my blood. I could recite every poem by Henry Wadsworth Longfellow, Maine's poet laureate, by heart.

By the shores of Gitche Gumee,
By the shining Big-Sea-Water,

Stood the wigwam of Nokomis,

Daughter of the Moon, Nokomis

In spite of my love for the state, I always felt like an outsider, a second-class citizen. My dad wasn't a banker, like I imagined all my friends' dads were. He was a grocer. Not only did he *not* go to an Ivy League college, he didn't even go to high school. And our skin was dark, and our hair was black, and our voices carried all the way to Newfoundland.

Because I didn't have blonde hair, a ski-jump nose, and freckles, I worked really hard at being liked. I was voted Homecoming Queen at Deering High School. At our yearly high school variety show, I was the headliner, performing solo comedy routines à la Carol Burnett. I dated the captain of the baseball team, and both of us were voted most popular. I defined myself as an "actress." I couldn't play tennis, couldn't ski, couldn't skate, couldn't swim or play bridge, but I was funny.

Here is an entry from my diary when I was twelve: *I love acting. I want to grow up to be an actress. If I do really good with my grades, maybe my parents will let me act.*

Clearly I flunked grammar, but the rest of my grades were passable, because at thirteen, I was cast in my first professional play at the Kennebunkport Playhouse, in Kennebunkport, Maine. The New York touring company of *South Pacific*, starring Penny Fuller as Nellie, used locals in the supporting parts. I was chosen to play Liat, the Polynesian princess.

A swarthy Armenian was the closest thing to a Polynesian princess they were going to find in the state of Maine.

To compensate for my ethnic insecurities, I found a hobby that allowed me to be anything I wanted to be. I had an active imagination. I spent most of my childhood in the attic in my house, and although this fact makes me sound like the crazy woman in *Jane Eyre*, I was what you might call a gregarious loner. The only place I felt safe to live out my fantasies was in the attic.

I dreamed of being on Broadway. Chita Rivera was my idol. I had seen her annually in San Juan, Puerto Rico, where my family had a condominium. She appeared at the El San Juan nightclub, in her own show, with three backup singers. I was mesmerized and bolstered by the fact that someone who didn't look like Sandra Dee could have a career in the theatre. Chita was exciting and brash and dark and funny— everything I thought I was or could be.

After graduating from high school at age eighteen, I left Maine to attend Stephens College in Columbia, Missouri. I couldn't wait to travel far away from my provincial home turf. Being a mediocre student in high school, I had few options for my secondary education. I had read that Stephens College had a fabulous theatre program. Tammy Grimes, the Unsinkable Molly Brown, was a graduate. That was enough for me.

I lasted one year at Stephens. The student body looked like Miss Missouri and her fifty-three runner-ups. I looked like Olympia Dukakis. The college was gated, and an adult female made the rounds at night, taking roll call. I felt constrained and rebellious. I ran away, was put on social probation, and then transferred to Emerson College in Boston. I was a small-city girl in a big collegiate town, which included Harvard, Radcliffe, BU, Boston College, and Northeastern. The city was alive and exciting and stimulating and dangerous for a girl searching for her identity. And there were no gates. None. The city was an open pasture for promiscuity. I soaked in love wherever I could find it.

An affair with my French lute teacher led to a year at the Sorbonne, where I fell in love with a Moroccan engineering student, which led to six months in Fez, where I stayed with his family, all of us sharing one room where we slept on mats on the floor, which then led to another year in Paris, where I fell in love with an Israeli soldier while studying mime with Jacques Lecoq at his École du Mime, which led to a final year at Emerson, where, in 1969, I finally graduated with a bachelor of science in speech and theatre.

I don't remember studying much while I was at Emerson. I remember acting classes, alongside Henry Winkler, who later became a superstar as Fonzie on *Happy Days,* and I have wonderful memories of Emerson's program at Deertrees Theatre in New Hampshire, where one summer I performed Nancy Twinkle in a production of *Little Mary Sunshine* and Simonne the servant in the light summer fare *The Persecution and Assassination of Jean-Paul Marat as Performed by the Inmates of the Asylum of Charenton*

Under the Direction of the Marquis de Sade, more commonly known as *Marat/Sade.*

The day after graduating from Emerson, I took a train directly to New York City. I bought a *Backstage* magazine in which I read that there was an open call for the national touring company of *You're a Good Man, Charlie Brown.* Miraculously, two weeks out of college, I landed the part of Lucy and got my equity card. I toured the United States with a group of actors who were mostly from Canada. On the road, I fell in love with the actor playing Linus. Lucy sleeping with Linus—Charles Schulz would have been horrified. But we were discreet. What happens on the back of a tour bus stays on the back of a tour bus. I followed him to Toronto, where he was from. Soon I fell in love with Canada too.

It happened that fast, my love affair with Canada. I crashed at Linus's pad at Bloor and Clinton Streets one night in July 1970, and I stayed. I unpacked my bags, cashed in my US unemployment cheque, walked to Honest Ed's, where I bought a set of steak knives for $4, and set up house.

Toronto was a melting pot of nationalities. I felt like I belonged. I immigrated to Canada in 1970—actually, to Niagara Falls, where I crossed the border in a barrel (anything to get some film on myself), and I became landed. Back then it was easy. All you needed was $50 and a free weekend to trap fur.

Linus and I and another young actress lived together on Clinton Street on the second and third floor of a tiny, dilapidated semi-detached wooden house. Dried remnants of grass mixed with broken beer bottles made up our front lawn. The first floor of the house was inhabited by a couple who were drunk most of the day and homicidal most of the night. We could hear her screaming for her life as he smashed chairs against the wall that were clearly meant to smash her. I'm not sure why we stayed in these treacherous surroundings, nor why we never called the police. The three of us were in our twenties, naive, and self-consumed. This ongoing domestic abuse only added colour to our already colourful existence trying to be actors.

The second floor of our apartment consisted of two small rooms, a kitchen, and a sitting room–cum–living room. The third floor, the attic, where we slept, had two tiny rooms with slanted ceilings that prevented even me at five foot two from standing up. There was just enough space for a double bed, or should I say double mattress. We spent many a cozy night in the small, hot, unventilated front room, where we sat on the floor, eating out of a fondue pot. Linus wrote songs and serenaded me with his guitar. We took up a lot of space with our simmering youthful romance. Our roommate, a beautiful young ingenue, kept quietly to herself.

We all lived together for a year until I returned to Paris, and Linus and I went our painfully separate ways. The pretty ingenue eventually gave up acting, but Linus has had a successful career in Canada for over forty years now. When we run into each other, it's always a lovely reminder to me of my beginnings in Toronto.

I've driven by Clinton Street a few times since leaving there in 1971. Not much has changed. The house is still there, and the grass out front seems a little greener. It's a wonder the house has never been torn down and another home built in its place. It still looks so shabby.

I parked my car in front of the house just recently, and a sea of memories came pouring in:

My first agent, Michael Oscars, who I met within a week of landing in Toronto. I walked into his office, introduced myself, and he signed me on the spot. In fact, he's been my agent for over forty years, and our relationship is the longest I've had with a man outside of my father.

My first commercial, for Kit Kat, in which I was directed to hold the candy bar, look directly into the camera, bite the candy, chew the candy, and meow, all on the count of thirty.

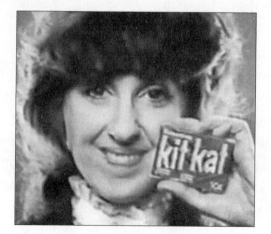

My first part in a movie, Ivan Reitman's film *Foxy Lady*, in which I appeared semi-nude. (Don't rush out to find it; the film is out of print, thank God.)

My first car, an orange Volkswagen convertible, which appeared back in my life thirty-five years after I had sold it. The present owner had tracked me down. She told me the car had been in her garage for years and she was about to sell it. She called to ask if I wanted to buy it back. I considered it. I'm as sentimental as they come. I finally declined the offer. I was living permanently in New York at the time and had no use for the car.

My introduction to pot, at Rochdale, a hippie high-rise on Bloor Street.

My first live Canadian stage show, in 1972, *Godspell*.

After leaving *Godspell*, and over the course of my career, I performed in almost every province across Canada. I acted in dinner theatre productions of *Vanities* and *Not Enough Rope* in Toronto, appeared in *Private Lives* with Maggie Smith and Brian Bedford at the Stratford Festival, was cast in the Charlottetown Festival production of *Anne of Green Gables* (a rite of passage for any Canadian actress), and was a regular on CBC's variety show *The Hart and Lorne Terrific Hour*, starring Hart Pomerantz, who later became a successful lawyer in Toronto, and Lorne Michaels, who went on to produce *Saturday Night Live*. I toured British Columbia in a Chrysler industrial show with Martin Short and his soon-to-be wife, and my soon-to-be sister-in-law, Nancy Dolman. I performed in *Salvation*, a rock musical in Winnipeg. I filmed the TV variety series *The Sunshine Hour* in Halifax with Eugene Levy and Joe Flaherty, and hosted, along with Dame Edna, *Just for Laughs* in Montreal.

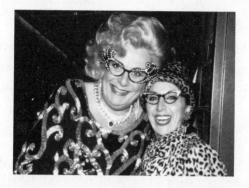

I even performed, with Marty Short, in the Canadian Opera Company's *The Glove,* in which we travelled extensively throughout Ontario, singing our hearts out as Leo and Leona Lion. By then my career was taking off and I was well entrenched in Canadian show biz. My biggest break came in 1975, when I auditioned for and was cast in Toronto's Second City stage show. In 1976, John Candy, Catherine O'Hara, Joe Flaherty, Harold Ramis, Eugene Levy, Dave Thomas, and I, all Second City performers, collaborated to create a television show called *SCTV.* My first twelve years in Toronto saw me marrying Bob Dolman, a Canadian writer, giving birth to our two sons at St. Michael's Hospital, and living in a beautiful home in High Park. Even Sharon,

Lois, and Bram wanted me for their *Elephant Show*. I would have stayed in Toronto forever if the success of *SCTV* hadn't brought our family to Los Angeles in 1986. For the next twenty-three years, I set up residence in Los Angeles and New York, but I longed to be back in Canada. (In September 2009, I took the plunge and bought a little house once again in Toronto. And so I've come full circle.)

With the exception of the explosion of cars and people, traffic jams, condominiums, and the epidemic of raccoons, the city of Toronto is as welcoming as it was when I first arrived. But now I see beavers on my lawn, and geese and ducks and otters and swans. I lead an enchanted life, on a pond in High Park. It's a perfect life, really. I'm even cohabitating nicely with a family of raccoons, in Toronto's west end, where it all began.

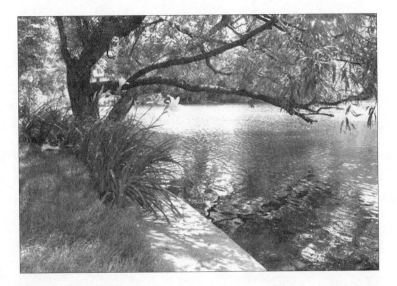

Armenia

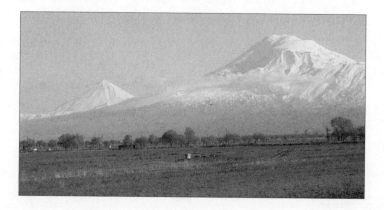

For the longest time I wished I were Jewish. First of all, I look the part. You know, big nose, dark eyes, pushy. Second of all, the Jews I hung out with—Mark Finks, my first boyfriend; Dr. Ralph Heifetz, my pediatrician; and Janet Shur, my super-confident best friend—had a good time being Jewish. They owned who they were. They had so much self-esteem. Unlike me. My parents, Sybil and John Martin, had gone to great lengths to assimilate and bury our ethnic, Armenian identity. I'm a distant cousin to Cher, Mike Connors, Charles Aznavour, and Clarabell the Clown, they told me. Why couldn't they have stopped at Cher? And you know who else? Arlene Francis from *What's My Line?* "Is it larger than a breadbox? *Haw haw haw.*"

As late as 1991, when I decided to write my first one-woman show, I didn't know where to find Armenia on a map. I thought it was a distant land that shipped frozen baklava to the corner deli. In fact, food was the only thing I associated with being Armenian. How was I going to write a one-woman show if I didn't know my roots? Who was this "one" woman who was about to reveal everything about herself? Up until that point in my career, I had been playing characters, hiding in glasses, hats, wigs. Could I be on stage as myself without all my props and feel that I was enough? There was only one way to find out. I booked a flight to Armenia.

"Jesus Christ, Andrea! Why do you want to go there?" my father asked as he grew more impatient and agitated by our conversation.

"Because I want to find out what it means to be Armenian, Daddy."

"You won't find it out over there. The people are poor. The country is dirty. They have nothing." He was angry. "Besides, your family came from Turkey and they're all dead."

Obviously, I knew *nothing* about my past. I went to the library and checked out everything ever written by, for, and about Armenians.

My dad was right. Historic Armenia was once a huge

and prospering land that stretched between the Black and Caspian Seas to eastern Turkey. But all that remained of Armenia today, after years of invasions by the Romans, Persians, Arabs, Mongolians, and Turks, was this small Communist-ruled republic. Armenia: population 3 million. A tiny republic occupying eleven thousand square miles of the southwestern tip of the Soviet Union, surrounded by Georgia, Azerbaijan, Iran, and Turkey.

But wait. Armenia was the first nation in the world to adopt Christianity. That was impressive. I kept reading with growing awe and fascination. Armenia, where Noah landed his ark. Armenia, where the alphabet was invented. A proud race of survivors that had lived three thousand years. Survivor. I liked that word. It made me feel courageous. A brave crusader, right up there with Tigran the Great. Maybe I had been selected by some divine power to put Armenia back on the map. If Cher (Sarkisian!) wasn't going to jump on the bandwagon, then maybe I should. Fonda had Vietnam, Sting had the rainforest, but Armenia was still up for grabs. I closed my eyes. I saw my face on a stamp.

I prepared for my trip. I contacted Armenians, who then gave me names of more Armenians to contact. Where had they been hiding all this time? Every Armenian I met wanted to help. I had more names that ended in "ian" in my address book than were listed in Fresno's city directory. My bag was packed with "souvenirs" I was told to bring: Bic lighters, bubble gum, decks of cards, costume jewellery, scarves, coffee, toilet paper, Handi Wipes, children's clothes, toys, and eight-by-ten glossy pictures of myself. The last item was important, they said. "You are a famous Armenian. People will be proud."

By the time I boarded the plane, I looked like Margaret Mead about to document the Samoans. I was carrying a video recorder, a mini cassette player, and a thirty-five-millimetre camera. I was excited. I was hopeful. I knew that when my feet touched Armenian soil, I'd be home.

Here and now I would like to rewrite Thomas Wolfe: "You can't go home a first time."

When my feet did touch land, nineteen hours later, all horrifyingly spent on the Devil's own airline, Aeroflot, I was just thankful to be alive. Flies buzzed inside the plane, pieces of ceiling dangled overhead, seat belts didn't fasten, and a flight attendant slept throughout the trip. Just before we took off, two pilots staggered up and down the aisle. I was sure they were looking for the cockpit. But not one of the three hundred Armenian passengers I was travelling with complained. In fact, they seemed happy. Men stood in the aisles, chain-smoking, laughing. Women sat in heavy coats guarding their bags. People sang. They were returning home to their loved ones. And I was an American girl, recording the event. I had never been around so many Armenians before. We had similar features, the same colour skin. But we seemed worlds apart.

It took four hours to get through customs. Armed Russian soldiers stood behind glass partitions. On the trip from the airport to the hotel I saw lambs being slaughtered at the side of the road, barefoot children sleeping in makeshift houses, and decaying buildings left unfinished in 100-degree heat. And everywhere I looked there were rocks. I knew that Armenia was called "the land of stones," and that only 10 percent of the country was covered by forests, but it seemed so barren and bleak. And backward. Peasant women in shapeless, worn clothes sat on the ground selling yogourt and melons. Men pushed underfed cattle down the middle of the road. Traffic was at a standstill.

And nothing seemed funny to me. A one-woman show? Every comedic bone in my body was broken. I didn't know what I'd expected, but this certainly wasn't it. All my life I had felt like an outsider. Too ethnic for Maine. Too ethnic for Hollywood. And now I was too waspy for Armenia. The Annette Bening of the Caucasus.

When we arrived in Yerevan, the capital, I clung desperately to my fading ideals. The city, one of the oldest in the world, seemed to be big and thriving, and I'd always thought of myself as a big-city girl. I hoped I might feel more at home. I got to the hotel and called some of the names on the lists I'd been given.

Greta, the fifty-year-old sister of a friend of a friend I had met in Los Angeles, was the first to arrive. She came with gifts of peaches and bread, and her dictionary, thank God. My only way of communicating was through mime. But aside from walking in place and pulling imaginary rope, I wasn't much good at making myself understood through visuals alone. Greta, a physicist, was unmarried and lived with her brother, his wife, their one-year-old child, and her mother in a small walk-up flat in the city. She seemed so happy to see me. She hugged me and said, "My English is poor, but I like very much to try." She apologized for not having a car. But there was a shortage of fuel, and automobiles were scarce, she said. She then took me by the hand and escorted me through the city, all the while speaking slowly, and searching for words in her little book.

"You should see Armenia before the earthquake. Before the massacres in Baku and Karabakh. Here are many refugees. We are overcrowded. We live with blockades and corruption. Since perestroika, we don't know what to believe. And now you see problems everywhere. But Armenia is beautiful country. You will find new energy here."

She showed me stone monuments of Armenian battles and bronze statues of Armenian heroes, and proudly pointed out massive pink buildings made from tufa, the national stone.

"It is a wonderful rock," she said, "our country's main source of wealth." I could see that the city had once been beautiful. But now, in striking contrast to these magnificently crafted "symbols" jutting up into the sky, were the shocking realities of everyday Armenian life. No food in the markets, just the occasional slab of fat in an unrefrigerated case. Empty cafés. No medicine. A few dreary, cheaply made clothes and shoes for sale. The opera, theatre, and museums were closed.

"It is too hot in August," Greta said, "to watch anything inside." People stood idly by on the streets, shaking their heads, many with blank stares. I recognized the faces. They looked no different from the faces of my ancestors who had fled their homeland a hundred years ago. Little had changed. There were few tangible reminders of a flourishing civilization that once had given birth to the most distinguished artists, musicians, and intellectuals in the world. *How could anyone live here?* I thought. Life seemed so impossible.

For the next ten days I submerged myself in the country. Armenians gave me food when they didn't have any, drove me in cars which they had to borrow. Everyone welcomed me. They showed me how proud they were to be Armenian and how important it was for me to feel that way too. I was shown ancient pagan temples, monasteries from the twelfth century, and churches all hand-carved out of stone.

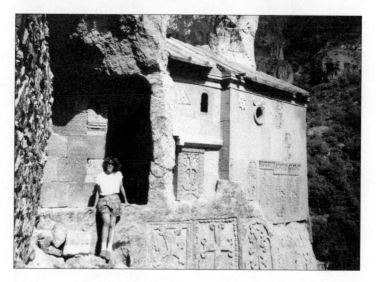

There were four thousand churches still standing in Armenia today, I was told. I was overwhelmed by each Armenian's knowledge of the country's history, and grateful and exhausted by their hospitality. "I vant to be alone," I soon found out, was not part of the Armenian vocabulary.

We spent evenings talking and philosophizing about the Turks, Communism, seventy years of an evil regime, and the future of the country. They wanted an independent Armenia, and were fighting for it. The newly elected president was on their side. It might take years. But they were prepared. They had no other choice.

I grew to love these people and their undying spirit. And I began to find my humour again, and to understand theirs.

"Do you know what makes an Armenian laugh?" Samvel Shahinian asked me during a dinner he had prepared for me one night. He was an artist and theoretician; his beautiful and gracious wife, Gulnara, was the head of Yerevan's Department of Foreign Affairs.

"What?" I asked, hoping that the door to our mutual comedy psyches might finally be unlocked.

He held his hand up and moved his little finger back and forth. I laughed.

"See," he said, "anything."

I asked him how Armenians could find humour in the terrible conditions in which they were forced to live, and he replied, "Because, you see, things cannot get much worse."

I began to see courage in each and every Armenian, the kind of courage I had never known: that despite the terrible hardships and living conditions, they still woke up with their dreams. I asked why they didn't leave and come to America, where they could have a better life. And they answered simply, with a quiet dignity and resolve, "If we go, there will be no Armenia."

By the time my trip ended, I was anxious to get home. I missed my kids. All lines to the United States had been cut off for a week. I wanted to take a shower. I wanted to sleep in a rodent-free room. I also wanted a cup of real coffee. Armenians received theirs from Russia, caffeine-free. The government, I was told, controlled all "drugs."

Greta and her brother drove me to the airport. We were silent all the way. As we stood outside customs, Armenians pushed and yelled and crammed their way past us. Greta apologized for their behaviour. "They are animals," she explained, "because no one has come to show them how to do better." Self-reliance had to be taught to Armenians again. Everyone knew this. I wanted to believe that nothing could destroy our race. If we had survived three thousand years, I hoped we could survive three thousand more.

I returned to Los Angeles on August 16, 1991, one day before the Soviet coup. I felt privileged to have been in Armenia while the next chapter in its history was being written. After seventy years of Soviet rule, Armenians were finally free.

* * *

Four years later, I was sitting on a plane that was flying from Los Angeles to New York, where I was about to open my one-woman show. A woman sat beside me. I didn't hear her or speak to her or see what she was reading, but I smelled a familiar smell. I turned to her and said, "Excuse me, are you Armenian?"

She could barely speak English but understood the word "Armenian" and nodded yes. What I really wanted to say was, *You smell like my grandmother. Can I hug you?* Then it dawned on me: I had studied everything about my ancestors, but I knew nothing about my own family. I couldn't recall one word of my own grandmother's. She had lived with us for twenty-six years in the room next to mine and I could not recall one conversation we had had together.

It was my mother who told me that Nanny had been brought to America when she was fifteen, in a pre-arranged marriage, and had six children with a man she never loved, a man twice her age. She had lost her father and brothers in the genocide, and had to leave her mother behind. She could never return to her homeland. I remember her sitting for hours, always wearing black, knitting and staring out the window. I remember wanting to make Nanny happy. But I couldn't. I was a child and I didn't understand. So I ran away from that sadness. Ran all the way up Mount Ararat for God's sake, looking for Noah's ark.

For the next five hours, I treated the woman next to me

like my own grandmother. I propped her feet up with pillows, put cushions behind her back. When the flight attendant asked her what she wanted for breakfast, and she said, not understanding, "Okay," I spoke for her. I said, "She'll have the steak and the omelette, and bring her a mimosa, she's had enough coffee." We toasted, neither one of us knowing what each other was saying. "Aaaah," we said, nodding our heads in agreement. We laughed. "Aaaah."

Then right before we were about to land, a phrase I hadn't heard since I was a child came back to me.

"*Tza vet danem*," I said to the woman. Armenians say this to people they love.

"*Tza vet danem*," she said.

It means: Let me take away your pain.

I opened my one-woman show, *Nude Nude Totally Nude*, at the Joseph Papp Public Theater on April 6, 1996. There were many laughs in the show. But for the first time in my life, I dared to not get laughs. It took courage. Not the courage of Tigran the Great, but in my own way, I was defending my people by just getting up there. In my own way, I was preserving my culture, like my boyfriend Mark Finks had preserved his. There may not have been many Armenians in the audience, but getting onto that stage, I was surrounded by three thousand years of history. Like an actor playing King Lear for the first time, I was never alone but embraced by all those who played the part before me. Finally, I belonged. The part of me I'd cut off, I'd found.

"*Tza vet danem*," I was saying to the audience.

"*Tza vet danem*," I was saying to myself.

Let me take away your pain.

My One-Year Diary, 1958

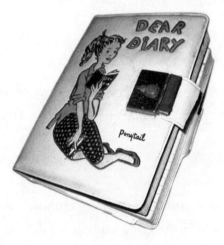

Property of andrea m.
189 Whitney Ave.
Portland, Me.

January 1, 1958

10 years old

When we were playing tag at school a boy came and pushed my pocketbook right off my hands and Mark F. said "Say your sorry to the young lady" and picked up my pocketbook.

January 2
The other girls were calling me a flirt because I liked Mark Finks.

January 11
I went to the Nathan Clifford Baked Bean Supper. I was very sorry that Mark wasn't there.

January 15
My birthday. 11 years old.
My mother didn't let me invite boys to my party because she thought I was to young. So I didn't have a very good one, even though it was fun.

January 17
Stephen R. sent me a birthday card on my birthday. Mark said that he was going to by me a ring but he never did.

February 1
I went to the movie Old Yellar today. I almost started to cry because Mark wasn't there and I was sick for the whole day.

February 4
I went to the Children's Theater today with my girlfriends and my boyfriend, Mark. He held my hand gently, and I was so happy.

February 19
Steven R. sent me a love note. The minute I read it I tore it up because I dislike him very much.

February 28
My dog Cinoman has been lost already for three days. Who knows when he is going to come back? All the rest of my family wants him not to come back but I do. We have looked every where and still not have found him and I have been awfly sad since.

March 7
Today I stopped piano and all my prevleges* will be taken away.

March 12
Today I went back to piano because I couldn't stand it anymore.

March 19
My doggie has not come back yet for three weeks and I don't think he ever will.

March 20
Today we got a cocker spaniel, which we had 30 minutes. The old woman was crying because she didn't have any children and the dog was just like one to her. So we gave it back.

---

* To this day, I still don't know how to spell priviledges, privaleges, priva-whatever

March 23

Today I went to the movie Sing Boy Sing starring Tommy Sands, with my Aunt and sister. It was a wonderful movie because it had alot of singing, loving, and alot of sadness and thats the kind of movie I like.

April 17

Today Steven G. and Stanley Sax were down my house. They came into the little brown hut with me. We talked for a little while then I suddenly fainted and fell on Steven. He put his arm around me and started to tap me lightly. After that Dear Diary, I am never going to try to faint again.

April 26

I went to Steven G. Splash party today at 8 to 11 oclock. I danced with Steven and Stanley the most times. It was the most wonderful party I have ever gone to in my entire life. (even though I am 11)

April 29

Today Mommy + Daddy came back from Florida and boy were they tan. They brought me back some shells for my rock collections, a very pretty dress, and last but not least a stuffed dog and I named him Cinoman.

May 16

Today after school Stanley and I were arguing about why he hated me and why Steven did. He got me so mad I ran away and started to cry. That was the first time I had ever started to cry when I was talking to a boy.

May 23

I found out the other reason that Stanley and Steven hate me. It is because I bounce to one boy to another. So I am going to try to be a lady even though I can't be.

May 31

Today nothing much happened except my father almost killed me for not coming home at seven oclock. He swore and did everything that was unnessersry.

June 12

Today I graduated from grammar school. I got 5 a's + 4 b's. I'll be in Jr. high school next year but I don't want to go because I'm going to St Josephs School (catholic). We have to wear a uniform every day. My parents are sending me because I talk to much, fool around with boys and I think they want me to get a better education.

July 4

Today was Cinomans birthday. But no Cinoman.

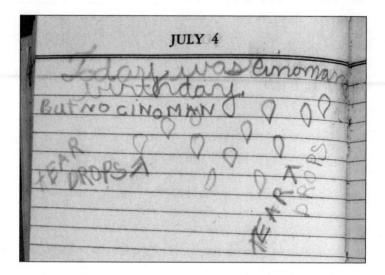

August 10

Today I went to Girl Scout Camp. But I didn't want to. I wanted to stay home and watch American Bandstand.

August 11

I'm at Girl Scout camp now. It is in the morning. We had oatmeal with raisons and it was terrible. I know I am going to lose 10 pounds. Everybody is a snob that is in my cabin. Even Jeanie V is as fresh as ever.

August 23

Today I came home from camp and boy I was glad. When I came home what a surprise I had. My American Bandstand yearbook was there. I know now that I am not going to camp next year.

September 6

Dear Diary

I saw the most wonderful picture in the whole wide world the other day. The name is Blue Denim. All about two teenagers who get in trouble, the girl becomes pregnant and they don't know what to do. They both come from good homes and they are very decent themselves. There afraid to tell there parents so they save up enough money so the girl can have an abortion. She is saved just in the nick of time because the boy finally tells the horrible truth. They get married at the end and live happily ever after. (They are 16 + 15.) Carol Lynley + Brandon de Wilde play the parts wonderfully. I saw it 7 times in a row.

September 11

I sent Dick Clark a letter and a picture I drew of him. But I think I sent it to the wrong address.

September 20

Today I think I started my period but I am not telling anybody. Not even my mother.

September 21

Today I dreamed that Steven slept over my house. When I was sleeping Steven called me over. I came over and he told me to sit on the bed with him and so I did that to. He kissed me and I kissed him back. Then he told me that he loved me. I said that I loved him and then he asked me to go steady with him.

October 12

I hate my mother + Nanna very much. All they try to do is cause fights. They let Marcie and Peter go to Aunties house but I had to stay home. And now I can't get out of the house until I make my bed. This morning Nanna made every bed in the house except mine while I was in church. And she expects me to make mine now.

December 31

I will always remember Mark F., Steven G, and until the day I die, Kenny Rossi. He is the most wonderful boy in the whole gosh darn world. God bless him forever. I love American Bandstand.

Memorandum

Jeanie Marcus and Janet Shur were almost my best girlfriends. They were smart, cute and not so poor either.

March 26, 1959

12 years old

Today is the first time I have written in my diary for a long,

long time. I had been so busy I had forgotten all about it. I think I'm going to get a new diary and start from the start, but I'm still going to keep this one.

And so I did. Kept it for fifty-seven years.

It's been that long since I've taken the diary out of the locked metal security box that sits on a high shelf in my closet. The box holds baby books, locks of the kids' hair, their first teeth, their first cloth bibs, their first baby brush, birth certificates, school evaluations, and their first pairs of hand-knit booties. I was rummaging through it the other day in hopes that I would find something that would inspire me to write. And there it was. My little plastic and pink (but now slightly dirty) diary with an embossed design on the cover of a ponytailed teenage girl writing in *her* diary.

It came with a clasp and a lock and, at one time, a tiny key. But over the years I had lost the key, so the diary remained unopened. I held it in my hand and then hugged it close. It was as if I'd found a bottle with a message inside it, a message that had been lost at sea for half a century and had now found its way back to me for a reason. What were the pages going to reveal to me about my childhood? Had I uncovered a pirate's bounty and was about to strike literary gold? Were secrets that I had hidden from everyone about to be unearthed? Was I going to find clues as to why I had spent a lifetime of uncertainty? Would Freud have had a field day with my innocent confessions?

I took out a pair of scissors and cut the clasp.

I read it from cover to cover, hoping to unlock some juicy tidbits. But nothing stood out as titillating *or* heinous. It seemed that nothing out of the ordinary happened in my eleventh year on this earth. And yet I wasn't disappointed. Strangely, I was relieved. I wanted to climb inside the pink plastic covers and get to relive that year all over again.

I remembered the term "boy crazy" and how often it was used to describe me when I was growing up. And yet my "obsessions" with boys seemed so innocent on the page. One boy danced with me, one kissed me, one gave me his ring. Big deal. After all, it wasn't until I was twenty-one that I lost my virginity. I wish I had kept *that* year's diary. That experience could have filled an hour with Dr. Drew.

But at eleven, nothing extraordinary happened to me. I was brought up in the '50s, in a warm and loving, albeit strict, Armenian household, and was taught decent values and morals. Yes, I might have needed a little more attention from boys than other girls my age. But my need for attention created in me an overactive imagination that for years now has served me in a life in the arts. How many other eleven-year-old girls were developing the fine skill of convincingly pretending to faint in front of a boy, on cue? How many other girls at age eleven were compulsively drawing pictures of Dick Clark and sending them to the wrong address? Or obsessively watching *American Bandstand* every afternoon and dreaming that one day they'd get to slow dance with a "regular" on the show. Jonas Salk was dreaming about curing polio. And I was dreaming about slow dancing with a sixteen-year-old thug from Philadelphia.

Dick Clark passed away recently, and part of my childhood died with him. I would love to know where Mark Finks and Stanley Sax are today. I would like to make amends with them and tell them I didn't really faint. I would like to know where Cinnamon ended up. Years after he went missing, my dad confessed to me that he had given Cinnamon away to a farm because of the dog's incessant barking. I stopped piano lessons but to this day wish I had continued. And although I hated summer camp when I was eleven, I was hired as a counsellor at the Luther Gulick camp, Wohelo, when I was fifteen, and taught drama to kids every summer for years after that.

Blue Denim to this day is still my favourite movie.

Since my eleventh birthday, when I made my first entry in my first diary, I have written in hundreds of journals; scribbled ideas on hundreds of napkins, boarding passes, and magazine covers; and now, thanks to my iPhone, I leave long lists for future essays, in my Notes app.

But I have never had another pink diary with a lock and key.

I wonder if they make them anymore.

Afterbirth

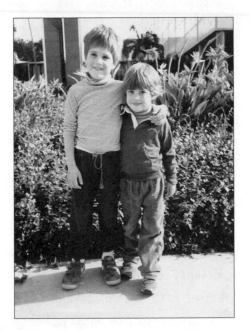

Recently, I accepted the invitation to write a monthly humour column for *ParentsCanada* magazine. What was I thinking? I don't remember my kids' names, never mind the way I parented them nearly thirty years ago. Except that I was anxious *all the time*. Worried that I was not doing it right, whatever "doing it right" is supposed to mean.

In 1986, when my sons were three and five, we moved from Toronto to Los Angeles. I enrolled them in a small private school that Meryl Streep and Dustin Hoffman sent their kids to. This only added to my anxiety. I would study Ms. Streep as she waved goodbye to her kids when she dropped them off in the morning, and feel that my goodbyes paled in comparison. Her goodbyes were the goodbyes of a real mother, so heartfelt, so honest, so underplayed. My goodbyes were empty, desperate, over the top. "Mommy loves you . . . MOMMY LOVES YOU." There wasn't a dry eye in the playground as Ms. Streep handed over the lunches to her kids and, with the brave determination of her Oscar-winning performance as Sophie, made the *choice* to get in her Volvo station wagon and drive away.

To overcompensate for my parenting insecurities, I volunteered my services at every school function from the time my kids were in preschool until they graduated from high school. And I'm not kidding—*every* school function. Every lousy school event that no one else signed up for, there was my name at the top. When your kids are growing up, you still believe the extra volunteer work you put in at their schools will somehow guarantee their future success and happiness. I really believed that a guidance counsellor or teacher or principal would remember that I had cleaned out the rabbit cages and, one day, would give my kid a great recommendation for Harvard. So with this insane belief, I emceed the comedy fundraisers, I raced in the bikeathons, jogged in the jogathons, boarded turtles and snakes at my home during school break, picked debris off the Santa Monica beaches, directed the school plays, and made cookies, lasagna, and Armenian bread and raffled them off along with my leopard-skin Edith Prickley hat. I drove the football, baseball, lacrosse, and tennis teams to every game, and spent thousands of dollars at silent auctions on bad crafts made by other well-meaning parents. I even participated, along with Ms. Streep and Mr. Hoffman, in the weekly storytelling hours. I hired a dialect coach and worked with him three times a week, not to be outdone by Ms. Streep and Mr. Hoffman. I recited *Wind in the Willows* with a German accent ("Vonce upon a time, there vas a vind in da villows") and *The Ugly Duckling* with a New York Jewish accent ("What do you want to do, shoot the ducklings, these lovelies?"). I acted out *The Velveteen Rabbit* as Ratzo Rizzo ("Hey, rabbits, I'm walkin' here. I'm walkin' here").

Of course, none of my volunteering did anything to secure my kids' places in the world. In fact, all it invariably did was make me more insecure as a parent. Volunteer work puts you in close proximity with other desperate parents, and then you start making small talk and digging for information, and the conversation moves to how many extracurricular activities your kids are involved in and what grades they got on a paper, and you soon find out that your kids are achieving far, far less than the other kids, and so besides spending endless hours making paper hats for the fall fair, you find out you really *are* a bad parent and your kids probably won't even graduate from preschool.

Babies and kids have a way of trumping everything. They have an uncanny effect on how we prioritize our lives.

When my oldest boy, Jack, was a mere three weeks old, I was flown to Los Angeles to be a guest on *The Tonight Show Starring Johnny Carson*. For a young actor starting out, an appearance with Mr. Carson was the most coveted spot on any talk show. If Johnny liked you, your career was launched overnight. None of this mattered to me as I sat in the green room with Jack, breastfeeding him, changing his diapers, rocking, walking, and attending to his every need. When I finally did my seven minutes with Mr. Carson, I was a resounding success. My only priority while I was on the panel was getting back to the green room for Jack's next feeding. I never once concerned myself with how I was coming across to *millions* of viewers. The conversation with Johnny consisted entirely of baby anecdotes. I joked with Mr. Carson that my doctor told me I was going to have twins but it just turned out to be a baby with a big nose. I said that Jack looked like Yoda when he was born, and although we thought he was beautiful, we also retouched his baby pictures. Okay, I admit that all those jokes were affectionately told at my child's expense, but in spite of using him as comic fodder on national television, he is today the most unconditionally loving son a parent could ever ask for.

In fact, Jack and my younger son, Joe, are my most astute critics, and I cherish their opinions. They make my career far more important than it is. The fact is, I don't think I would have had the career I've had if I hadn't given birth to my two sons. My kids taught me how to listen and how to love, and because of that, I believe I am a better actress. They have given me balance and perspective in a career that is too often all-consuming.

When Joe was about to start his last year of high school, I was offered the lead in a new Broadway musical—not my regular supporting part, but the lead, with a very lucrative contract. The show was called *Seussical*, based on the Dr. Seuss books, and I was to play the Cat in the Hat. However, rehearsals would start in September and I'd have to sign a nine-month contract. That meant I would miss Joe's entire last year of high school. Every time I pictured the curtain going up in New York, I thought of Joe, in Los Angeles. I would not be there for his football games, college applications, homecoming, the jazz ensemble, the high school musical, graduation—a year never again to be repeated. I would not be there for my son. I called my agent, who would have benefited greatly from my doing the part. And I will never forget what he asked me: "Andrea, would you rather be remembered as a great Cat in the Hat or a great mom?" I said no to the part. I stayed with Joe for his senior year, and I have never regretted the decision.

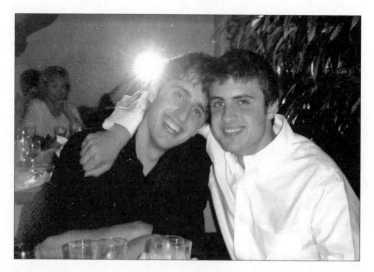

Jack (*left*) and Joe (*right*)

Today, my sons don't need me in the same way they did when they were children. Joe is an aspiring actor and a musician, and plays in a band. We both performed together recently in the TV series *Working the Engels*. I felt fortunate to be able to share the stage with my son. Jack is a music editor for films and collaborates with many film composers, including Hans Zimmer. My sons are both doing great. They don't need any interference from their mom. But I can't help thinking that if I drove Joe's band around, they'd get more gigs, or if I performed for Mr. Zimmer's Christmas party or even slept with him, Jack would get a bigger office.

I'd even throw in my Edith Prickley hat.

Birthdays

May 4 is my youngest son's birthday. As is customary, this year I bought him way too much and flew him round trip from Toronto to New York for a jam-packed, fun-filled, overly indulgent weekend. I bought him theatre tickets, wined and dined him at his favourite restaurants, slipped him some cash, and bent over backwards to honour his special day. I made his bed, bought him clothes, cooked for him, and never let him touch a dirty dish. I came very close to putting him in the bath and splashing him with bubbles. A bonded slave. What a martyr I am.

While he was opening his gifts, I asked him if he could remember his favourite birthday party over the years. He thought for a while, then said, "No, not one really stands out." I flashed back over all the years. Years of plastic cowboys on cakes, Chuck E. Cheese's outings, Disneyland, Knott's Berry Farm, sleepovers for way too many boys, pool parties where

I worried all night that someone would drown, Jacuzzi parties where I worried all night that someone would pass out, and then once, one kid actually did. (Thank God his mom was a close friend or I'd still be dealing with a heavy lawsuit.) Years of making small talk with parents as the kids arm-wrestled in the backyard, in the living room, on their beds, in the garage, on top of the car, and inside the trees. Years of bulk buying at Costco. Years of winning my son's approval. Did our family throw the best birthday party? Was the $50 videogame that each kid received in his bag of goodies a lovely parting gift, or a desperate, tacky plea for love and acceptance?

Birthdays. I tried to recall one of mine. And only two stood out. My twelfth, when Mark Finks, the freckled, red-haired Jewish boy who I had had a crush on for one year, finally kissed me, and my fiftieth, when one of my close male friends came to my party as a woman. He had just written to all his friends, his wife, and their two kids that he had been living a lie for fifty years. He had felt like a woman all his life, and he was finally going to have the operation to be one. My party was his first public outing. I was honoured that he felt safe enough with me to know he would not be judged, even with his stuffed bra, painted nails, and long, blown-out blonde hair.

Other than those two birthdays, every one is a blur. The routine dinners. The occasional family gatherings. These days, the trend among my wealthy friends is to throw elaborate birthday parties, renting a fabulous space in New York, hiring an orchestra, having original music written to commemorate their life, inviting top celebrities to sing about them in front of 250 of their closest friends, and paying hundreds of thousands of dollars for the memory.

At Sarah Jessica Parker's extravagant black-tie party at the Plaza Hotel, the women wore ball gowns, the men wore white tails, and twenty violinists serenaded us as waiters handed out buckets of caviar, lobster, and champagne. Then we all sat down for a six-course meal. At my darling Nathan Lane's black-tie dinner at the Rainbow Room, Mel Brooks, Elaine Stritch, Patti LuPone, and Matthew Broderick all performed. At Jane Fonda's sixtieth birthday extravaganza, Ted Turner, her husband at the time, gave her a cheque for a million dollars. Okay, yes, it would be hard to forget those birthdays. But even if I had an unlimited budget, I don't have that many friends. Twenty-five people in the Rainbow Room is pathetic.

My son is right. Not one of his birthday parties really stands out. In spite of all the hard work, the planning, the organizing, the gifts and gift bags, the entertainment, the money spent, the fretting over what would be the perfect party, I remember the details of only one: 8:31 a.m., May 4, 1983, St. Mike's Hospital, Toronto, Ontario, Canada. Dr. Wilfred Steinberg delivered our beautiful son, Joseph Martin Dolman, in natural childbirth, no complications. Weight: seven pounds, twelve ounces; length: twenty and a half inches.

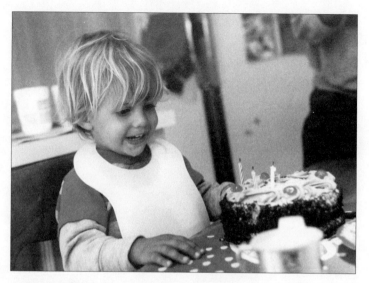

Happy birthday, Joe. That day I will never forget.

Dating #1

In 1991, I was a single parent with two young sons, ages six and eight. All my friends were married or were in relationships, and they constantly pressured me to date.

"Why aren't you dating? Why aren't you dating?"

I had no time for anything, least of all dating. But they persisted.

"Why aren't you dating? Why aren't you dating? You're attractive, you dress well, you're in show business. Hell, you had your own sitcom for two or three episodes. Why aren't you dating? Why aren't you dating?"

One morning, frustrated at the never-ending barrage of questioning, I sat down at my desk. This is the rant that followed.

Why Aren't I Dating?

Why aren't I dating? Why aren't I dating? Here's a typical day in my life. You be the judge.

(To be read without pausing.)

I get up at 5:00 a.m. I pour myself a cup of coffee, which is set the night before to brew at 4:45. I listen to my Deepak Chopra tape to release the powers of creativity and compassion within me. I open my chakras, I bless my toaster, I bless my ex-husband because if I don't the resentment will kill me, I breathe, I try on my jeans, I take off my jeans. I drink another cup of coffee. I walk around the block for a half an hour. I lift a couple of weights. Get the kids up. Make the kids breakfast. Help them with their homework, which they should have done the night before but I let them watch four hours of television instead because I'm a single parent and I'm guilt-ridden. I bluff my way through US history. I lie and say that Florida is one of the original colonies. I don't know. I never knew.

"Mom, Florida isn't one of the original colonies. What's the point of learning anything if you forget it when you're old?"

"Just suck back those Froot Loops," I say, "we're leaving in ten minutes, and call your father if you

wanna know about history. Ask him about the date he left me."

I have another cup of coffee, I pack the kids' lunches. Wash the dog's bowl, the cat's bowl. I read aloud from the New York Times *to secretly test the kids on their vocabulary. They know nothing. We're spending $30,000 a year on private education and they know nothing. Oh sure, they've been taught how to express their feelings. "Mom, don't humiliate me!" They just don't know how to spell it.*

I breathe, I try on my jeans, I take off my jeans, put on my sweatpants, load the kids into the car. Pick up another two kids. Drive in traffic for thirty-five minutes. Drop them off at school. "I love you boys! Have a great day!" Nothing. No response. A grunt. I blow them a kiss and they give me the finger. I put gas in my Isuzu Trooper, which I am driving because my Mustang convertible was stolen at gunpoint in front of my house. I stop at Starbucks. The woman in front of me orders a grande non-fat free-pour extra-hot no-lid cap. I say to myself, That can't be better than a goddamn cup of coffee. *I drive back home. It's only 7:45.*

I burn some incense. Ommmmmmm, I chant. I try on my jeans again. They still don't fit. I confirm the orthodontist appointment. The saxophone lesson. Cancel my massage because there's a conflict with my boys' baseball game, and I'm in charge of snacks so I have to be there. I plan tonight's dinner: chicken piccata in a pita and rice pudding. Possibly a fruit on the side. I read somewhere that a child has less chance of becoming a serial killer if you sit as a family and have dinner. I call my agent. He's in a meeting. I call my manager. She's in a meeting. I try on my jeans again. They still don't fit. I wear them anyway! I drive for two hours into the city for an audition for the voice of a spoon, which I don't get. They go with a blonde—go figure. It's not even noon. I'm hungry, angry, lonely, and tired. Why aren't I dating? If Brad Pitt came up to me and asked me out right now, I'd say, "Fuck you, asshole! Go inside and wash your hair!"

Dating #2

In 2003, I was *still* single. I decided to join an online dating service. I really thought I was going to meet my soulmate after one email exchange and suddenly find myself on the top of a mountain in Hawaii, making out with this guy in a bathtub like I was in a Cialis ad. Cialis, for erectile dysfunction. What the hell are those commercials saying? A guy can drag a bathtub up a three-thousand-foot mountain, but his penis he can't raise six inches? Anyway, after a month of obsessively checking my inbox, pardon the expression, I terminated the contract.

The truth was, I liked being single. I liked my freedom, I liked coming and going as I pleased. I had two full-grown sons who were finally out of the house, which meant I had a lot of free time to sit by the phone, waiting for them to call. Would it have killed them to pick up the phone once in a while? Had they forgotten they had a mother? Who did they think paid for the bar mitzvah? Why am I talking like this? I'm not even Jewish. This was the kind of message I left for them once a week: "Hi, boys! It's your mother. ANDREA MARTIN! We met while I was raising you. I thought we really hit it off. Listen, if you aren't presently seeing *another* mother, would you give me a call?" It was obvious I had to get a life outside of my children.

And then this happened.

His name was Terry. He was twenty-eight. I was fifty-seven. We fell in love.

Other than the time we went shopping together at Club Monaco, where the salesperson asked, "Would your son like to try on the khaki pants?" no one much commented on our age difference. And by "much commented," I mean to my face. Everyone seemed happy for me. God knows what was said behind my back, what conversations were struck up at Bar Centrale, an after-hours hangout for the Broadway elite. I'm sure many jokes were told at my expense among my close and loving friends. I mean, how could they help themselves? The twenty-nine-year age difference was comedy gold.

In spite of that, I knew my friends were relieved that I had finally met someone. Even my sons, now in their twenties, were encouraging: "Mom, you two seem sweet together." "Good for you, Mom." "Who cares how old he is as long as you're happy." Somewhere deep inside, they must have felt the burden of being my sons, my confidantes, my everything, was finally being lifted. They didn't have to take care of their mother and her feelings anymore. They could have their own lives and not feel guilty that their mom was alone.

Of course, I pretended I had a life. Little did they know that I was home alone, talking to myself, rearranging pillows on the couch, pacing around the living room in my bathrobe, checking my emails compulsively. And knitting. Constantly knitting. For them. In case it ever snowed in Santa Monica, California, and they needed thirty-eight handmade, worsted-wool fisherman-knit sweaters to keep them warm.

But back to Terry. My beautiful twenty-eight-year-old lover. And he was beautiful. Six foot five. Trim, handsome, muscular, an accomplished athlete. Graduated from an Ivy League school. Dear, kind, earnest. An aspiring actor.

We met while performing in a play together in Boston. It was his first acting job. Or to use the more current jargon, the first time he had ever been "booked." (I hate that word. Every time I hear an actor say, "I just got booked," I cringe. There is something so inherently ugly about this concept. Actors are artists, creative, fluid beings. Not petty criminals. Actors, show some self-respect, goddamnit.)

In any case, the play in which we had both been (booked) was a Christopher Durang comedy, in which I had the lead. I paid little attention to Terry other than to be polite. As the self-appointed Grand Dame of Legitimate Theatre, I was busy mentoring the entire cast with my upbeat personality and professional work ethic. Basically, I was way too self-involved to notice anyone, least of all this novice actor.

It had been fourteen years since I had dated anyone. During this time I hadn't even fantasized about falling in love. I'd given up on having a relationship. I believed the dating part of my life was over. I convinced myself that the one-night stands, the affairs, the orgies I had had in the '70s and '80s were more than enough for a lifetime. Hooking up with someone at this point was just plain greedy. And I was scared. In the fourteen years since I had been sexually active, so much had changed.

For instance, the use of condoms had become the norm. Not that I was unfamiliar with condoms. I remember experimenting with every kind of contraceptive when I was in my twenties and thirties, and always came back to the Trojan 4× Lambskin, I think they were called. They were very sheer and sticky and difficult to manoeuvre. They were packaged in a blue plastic cylindrical tube. You had to break open the seal by pulling the two ends of the cylinder apart. Most of the time, the seal wouldn't break, so you'd have to hit it on a table to loosen it, or use your teeth to pry it open, and eventually the tube would come apart, but by then it would be impossible to get it on a flaccid penis.

Another thing that had changed drastically in the four-teen years since I had dated was the hair on a woman's vagina. There wasn't any, or if there was, it looked like a landing strip of five sparsely cropped hairs. I still looked like an African bush woman down there. This new look on young women seemed aggressive and unwelcoming, like sleeping on pavement when you could be sleeping on grass.

I was clearly out of the sexual loop.

After six weeks in Boston, we finished the run of the play. Terry had been attentive, respectful, and professional. He never overtly flirted with me, or maybe he did but I was unaware. After our final performance, he came into my dressing room to say goodbye. He thanked me for everything he had learned while working on the play, and then said shyly, "I hope we get to see each other again."

"I'm sure we will," I said matter-of-factly. "You're so talented, and I know you're going to have a long career."

Terry continued. "Would you like to get a drink sometime? Can I call you when we get back to New York?"

"Terry, are you asking me out?"

"Yes," he said, "I find you very attractive."

"Dear God, I'm old enough to be your mother."

Terry reassured me. "I don't think of you that way."

"Oh, okay." I compulsively lined up my lipsticks while no longer making eye contact with Terry. He kept staring at me. Was it my turn to speak? I could no longer feel my body.

"Sure, well, sure, that sounds good, I mean, fun, sure, I'll call you. I have to go to Los Angeles for work, but I'll be back, and yes, coffee. Or a drink, or some food, or something would be good, why not? Call me, or I'll call you. I mean, okay, if you really want to. Sure, that sounds like it could be fun." I wrote down my number for him. Terry left the dressing room. I stood there, giggling uncontrollably. The giggles then turned to tears, the tears turned into giggles, and then, frozen in front of the dressing-room mirror, I devoured an entire box of Godiva chocolates.

After I returned from LA, a week later, Terry called me. He left messages that I played a hundred times, to myself, to my girlfriends. Terry, calm, genuine, confident. Andrea, nervous, shut down, insane. For weeks I made excuses as to why I was too busy to get together with him, until I finally got up enough nerve and asked him to my home. I didn't have any alcohol in the house. I'd stopped drinking fourteen years before. As much as I needed a bottle of vodka at 8 p.m., Wednesday, September 14, 2003, I made two cups of peppermint tea for yours truly, Miss Havisham, and her twenty-eight-year-old date.

Terry sat on the couch, and I, too scared to sit next to him, sat on the floor. We talked for a very long time. And then Terry asked if he could kiss me.

"*What?* Oh wow, kiss me? Gosh, I don't know, wow, kiss me, gee . . . Can I have a minute to think about that?" I walked into the kitchen, held on to the stove, counted to ten, and returned. "Okay, I'm ready, ask me again."

"I think we've lost our window of opportunity," he said.

"Oh, I'm so sorry. It's just been so long, and I'm so nervous, and I'm out of practice."

Terry stopped me. "Why don't we try this again another night and see how we do?"

"Sure," I said, "that would be great." I walked him to the door. He hugged me. It was nice, and awkward, as awkward as you can imagine a thirteen-inch height difference might be.

The next day, I went back into therapy. Ilona, my therapist, was encouraging. She saw nothing wrong with the age difference between Terry and me. She thought it was important for me to keep myself open to this new experience, however it turned out. She coached me. I took notes. We role-played. I felt prepared.

Terry and I had our second date, at my apartment, the following week. Again I made tea, but this time I sat on the couch *with* him, per Ilona's instructions. I'd rehearsed what I was going to do: kiss him when the moment was right. I wasn't listening as Terry talked. All I kept thinking was *Is this the right moment?* I had to strike while the iron was hot. I closed my eyes, leaned in toward him, and with the strength of Zeus and the charm of Medusa, I planted my mouth on his.

Terry was not thrown off guard but instead kissed me back tenderly. He held me close to him. We kissed for hours. We never took our clothes off. We rolled around on the floor and kissed some more. Hours and hours, holding, kissing, laughing. Me, a sober fifty-seven-year-old mother of two grown sons, in the arms of the dearest, most caring twenty-eight-year-old.

It didn't occur to me at the time that this relationship couldn't last. In the moment, in all the moments we had together, we were perfect. We dated for three months before we made love, another order from my therapist. In that time, we got to know each other, and out of that knowledge came trust. Terry waited patiently for "the day." We both agreed to take tests for sexually transmitted diseases, which came back negative. We were free to experience intimacy, and make love without having to break open a blue plastic cylindrical tube.

I think the first thought that pops into anyone's mind when they see a younger man and an older woman in a relationship is *What do they have in common? What does he see in her? How does she relate to him?* Terry and I were both innocents in many ways. Stuck in the same time zone. I had stopped growing emotionally by acting out in my twenties. And Terry, in his twenties, had a lifetime ahead of him to grow. He came into my life when I was ready to accept love. I came into his life when he was ready to give it.

After almost a year together, the relationship ended. It was inevitable. Eventually, the romance died down and the realities of a twenty-nine-year age difference appeared. Terry wanted to have children. And even though I fantasized about being pregnant at fifty-eight by carrying an egg from a donor fertilized by Terry's sperm, I knew we were meant to go our separate ways.

I was heartbroken when it ended. For one thing, having

sex while sober and present is powerful, and it created a profound bond between me and Terry. And I loved him. He was decent and kind. We had fun together. Terry wanted to remain friends. I needed time apart from him. I knew that one day we would reconnect.

I didn't sign up for a long-term relationship when I met Terry. My therapist made sure of that. *Stay in the moment. You'll know when it's time to move on.* It took me two years to get over Terry. Two years of reading poetry by Mary Oliver, two years of mourning over this young man.

I saw Terry again, four years after our relationship ended. He'd been "booked" in a play on Broadway, and I went backstage to say hello. He told me he was married and had a son. It's what he always wanted. Just recently I heard that he moved to Los Angeles and had given up acting. He's a fireman now. I love that. I hope he's happy.

As for me, I'm open to love again. I pray it doesn't take another fourteen years. But if it does, I still have several alpaca sweaters to knit for my sons.

My Mustang Convertible

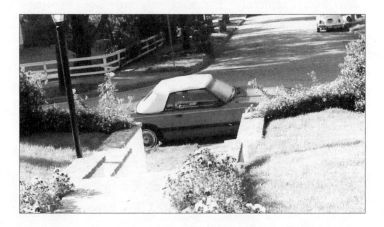

On an April morning in 1992, at 10 a.m. in broad daylight, I was held up at gunpoint in front of my house in Pacific Palisades, California. Pacific Palisades is a sought-out and, for most people, financially prohibitive, affluent neighbourhood snuggled between the more trendy Malibu and the diversely populated Santa Monica. It is serene, relaxed, and beautiful, if you're a Stepford Wife. Families with children love it. Little leagues abound. The air is clean because of the proximity to the ocean. There are churches on every street corner, and AA meetings in the corners of every church. But seldom do you see a person outside walking anywhere, or for that matter, outside at all.

I had just driven home after hiking for an hour and had parked my red Mustang convertible on the street in front of my house. I sat in my car while I listened to a pop song on the radio. I can't remember the exact song now, but I'm sure it was about a breakup, and it was sad and schmaltzy, the kind of gut-wrenching song I can listen to for hours. Don Henley's "Heart of the Matter" comes to mind. Whatever it was, I was singing along at the top of my lungs, drowning out my sorrows because of my own recent depressing breakup with a young and heart-stoppingly adorable boyfriend, and didn't notice a car had pulled up a few feet in front of mine. When I finally did look up, I saw a well-dressed young man, maybe eighteen or twenty years old, walking slowly toward me. He was smiling and seemed friendly. His companion waited by their car.

He approached my open window.

"Hi," I said cheerfully, like the spokesperson for the Pacific Palisades chamber of commerce. "What can I do for you on this fine day?"

"I like your car," he replied.

"Well, thank you," I said. "I like it too."

"I really like your car," he continued.

"Well, thank you. That's so nice of you to say." I was about to ask him into my house so I could draw him a map to the dealership when I sensed something was wrong.

I started to close the window, and as I did, the man pulled

out a gun. He stuck it through the opening and pointed it toward me, a few inches from my head.

"Get out of the car," he said.

"What?" I said.

"Get out of the car, *now.*"

Wait a minute. This is crazy, I thought. *Why is he raising his voice at me? What's going on? What have I done?* I was just being friendly, and now I was about to be on the evening news, the local evening news, but how bad could that be? I was in show business, after all, where any PR was good.

The young man held his gun to my head as he motioned to his buddy, who then menacingly walked toward us.

It was like a scene out of *CSI* or *Law and Order: SVU* or any of those episodic crime shows that I had never been cast in but had watched enough to know that had *I* been hired to play the girl in the Mustang convertible, my guest star arc was about to be over. These guys were not house hunting in the Palisades. They were not out for a morning drive. They were not lost. They did not need directions to the nearest Gelson's to buy chicken tenders and barbecued ribs. They were not selling chocolate bars to raise funds for their high school prom.

They wanted my car and, it seemed, were willing to kill me to get it.

I opened the door calmly and stepped out, and as I did, I noticed my Starbucks grande latte on the dashboard.

"Excuse me," I said politely. "Would you be kind enough to hand me that cup of coffee? I don't want it to spill all over my leather seats." That morning before my hike I had taken my Mustang to the Palisades car wash, where it was hand-cleaned and polished. "Detailed" in car-wash speak. It looked brand new, the tires sparkling, the dashboard smelling like California lemons just picked from a neighbourhood tree. It made me sick to my stomach to think that in a matter of minutes, my seats would be stained and soiled by my freshly brewed Ethiopian dark roast.

Shockingly, the gun-toting but accommodating car thief opened the door and obediently handed me my lukewarm skim latte. It was then that I saw my purse in the passenger seat. The next two hours flashed before me. I thought of all the phone calls I would have to make to cancel my numerous credit cards and the multitude of irritating recordings I would have to bypass in order to talk to a real human being, and likely not one with a compassionate ear. Then I'd have to phone and muddle through the bureaucracy of the Department of Motor Vehicles to reapply for a new driver's licence, even though, in a matter of minutes, I would no longer need one.

"I'm sorry to disturb you, sir," I said. "Can I ask you one more thing? Would you mind giving me my pocketbook? It's right beside you."

At that point, the second obliging hoodlum handed me my purse as he jumped into the passenger seat. Someone had taught these boys manners. I stood holding my latte in the middle of the street in the upscale neighbourhood of the Palisades, and before the director could yell "Cut!" they were off. Yes, Butch Cassidy and the Sundance Kid sped away in my red Mustang convertible and disappeared over the horizon forever.

It was 10 a.m., not a soul was to be seen, no witnesses to the crime, in this godforsaken ghost town. I ran into my unlocked house. I called the police. They arrived a few minutes later.

I told them the entire story. They said I was lucky that I had not been shot.

"Never ever engage in conversation with a person with a gun," the officer instructed. "You should have given them what they wanted and not said a thing. You were too trusting and naive. That was a stupid thing to do. You're lucky to be alive."

That afternoon I had all the locks to my house changed and a $2,000 alarm system installed. I used it responsibly for a couple months but never learned how *not* to set it off every time I opened a window, so I stopped using it completely.

My Mustang was found a few weeks later in south-central Los Angeles during the Rodney King riots, stripped of anything that could be sold. The young men—not experienced thieves, the cops had told me—had followed me to my home, where they had planned to steal my car, and then had taken it for a joyride and abandoned it. There was nothing left of the car to salvage. It was beyond repair.

Over the years, I have shared this story with a few people, and the first thing they say to me, surprisingly, is not "Thank God they didn't kill you" but "Never buy a red car. You're a moving target, for both thieves *and* cops."

The next car I bought was an Isuzu Trooper. It was red. I

couldn't help myself. Until I sold it, though, I stayed under the radar. No traffic violations, nor was I ever held up at gunpoint again while someone helped himself to my shiny SUV.

I loved my Isuzu Trooper. It was a roomy, robust, family car and functioned for many years as a carryall for my two growing sons. After my Mustang was stolen, I settled into being a practical mom with a practical car. The days of driving up the coast of Malibu alone in my sexy red convertible when the kids were in school, my hair blowing in the wind, me wailing along with Queen's "Bohemian Rhapsody"— those beautiful little escapades were over. That terrifying incident robbed me not only of my Mustang but also of the youthful exuberance that went with owning it.

I live in New York and Toronto now. I no longer have a car. When I visit my sons in Los Angeles, I rent one. I always rent a convertible. Of course, I ask if they have a red one, but they always seem to be out. I load the boys, now in their thirties, into the car and we drive up the coast, laughing and singing and having a glorious windblown time. In fact, no matter what's going on in my life or theirs, the convertible has always provided us with an instant bond, and an intoxicating distraction.

I miss my car. I miss my youth. I miss being a naive, free-spirited mom.

But I'm grateful. As the cops said, I'm lucky to be alive . . . but never more alive than when I can get behind the wheel of a red Mustang convertible, pack up all my troubles in an old kit bag, and drive, drive, drive.

Why I Fly to Atlanta
to Get My Hair Cut

2013

The day started out uneventfully. That's what I like when I travel. Unevents. I went to bed early, at 10:30 the night before, so that I could get my delicious seven hours of sleep before the alarm went off at 5:30. I had two cups of coffee, obsessed about what I was going to wear, and then settled on my breathable Lycra pink jeans, hip and yet comfortably roomy, for the two-hour flight to Atlanta, Georgia, where I was travelling that day to get my hair cut. Twelve hours later, I would be taking the two-hour return flight back to New York.

I had the drill down pat. After all, I had been making this trip every six to eight weeks for the last twelve years.

I wore my Skechers backless, slip-on sneakers so as not to take unnecessary time at security, packed my computer in hopes that I'd write a chapter for my book, and carried a little purse just big enough for a passport and a Luna bar.

I took the elevator down to the first floor of my apartment building, where at 7 a.m. Raphael, the doorman, hailed me a cab. Within two seconds, one miraculously appeared. There was no traffic on the way to LaGuardia. The taxi driver took a shortcut and I arrived twenty minutes later at Terminal B. There was no line at the AirTran counter or the machine at which I printed my boarding pass; no line through security; no line in the women's washroom; no line at Au Bon Pain; no line at the gate, where I boarded early; and no line on the runway. Ours was the first plane to take off. There was even an empty seat next to mine. The flight attendants were cordial, gave me three packages of Biscoff cookies instead of the usual meagre one, and no one lowered his or her window shade or slept with earphones on, the loud music leaking out to annoy me. Even the coffee tasted remarkably like coffee. It was a particularly good day to fly. There was not a cloud in the sky, no rain or snow in the forecast. Everything went smoothly. It was a sign, an omen, I thought. The universe was cheering me on. *You go, girl. There's nothing remotely insane about you travelling 881 miles south down the eastern seaboard to get your hair done.*

"Get changed," said the beautiful, petite, smiling Urie, hair assistant extraordinaire.

I lay down on the chaise longue adjacent to the shampoo sink, my little white robe wrapped loosely around me, closed my eyes, and melted into the soft brown leather. After a ten-minute scalp massage by his doting assistant, the master coiffeur, Pascal, appeared and took over. His adroit hands and astute eyes would soon transform my grey roots to a gorgeous Salma Hayek brown, refresh my highlights to a sun-kissed Jennifer Aniston gold, and thin out my layers from a Tina Turner shag to a tousled yet kempt Penélope Cruz. My hair would then be luxuriously blown out. Four hours later I would be back on the plane to New York, and asleep in my apartment by ten. I would be exhausted but feeling beautiful. It was a fair trade-off.

I live in New York and Toronto, but it doesn't matter where I live, really, because wherever I am when my hair needs to be done, I fly to Atlanta. I have travelled there from Los Angeles in the middle of shooting a TV series, from Seattle in the middle of a tryout of a Broadway musical, from Newfoundland while shooting a film, from Williamstown while performing a play, from Florida while visiting my dad, from Maine while hiking the trails of Arcadia. Regardless of where I am, if it is time to get my hair cut, I board a plane for Atlanta. That's where my hairstylist lives and works. Pascal Bensimon is his name. Pascal, of Pascal Bensimon Haute Coiffure.

His salon is in a little detached house in a residential area of the conservative, old-money neighbourhood of Atlanta called Buckhead. The salon has four rooms, the walls decorated with colourful, original art from France. It has a working fireplace; a kitchen in which salads and sandwiches are prepared; an expensive espresso machine; freshly grated ginger for hot ginger tea, a specialty of the salon; comfortable brown leather lounging chairs; a computer and printer at one's disposal; a porch with wicker chairs to sit on while one waits for her colour to take hold; two darling, dedicated young assistants; never more than three or four clients; and Pascal, the messiah, holding court as he cuts and colours the hair of his female devotees. He runs his Israeli/ Moroccan/Parisian hands through each woman's hair, massaging their heads and shoulders, kissing their cheeks, smiling and listening intently to every word they say. Each woman whose hair is caressed and styled by Pascal believes she is the most beautiful woman alive on the planet. He is the Houdini of Hair, and every woman who meets him is under his spell.

I met Pascal at a West Coast spa in 2002. We were both guests during one of its four coed weeks. He was there by himself, as I was. He was adorable, with unruly wavy dark hair that somehow managed to look stylish no matter how much sweat was pouring down his olive skin. He had magnetic charm and an introspective demeanour, and his emotions ran the gamut. He was quiet on the hikes, mischievous in cardio boxing, weepy during yoga, frisky in the pool, shy at dinner. He was mysterious. He stood out at this coed week because he was single and forty. The typical man that came to the coed week came with his wife, and the average age of the couple was sixty-five.

I had been a regular guest at the spa for over ten years and had never met anyone like Pascal. I had hiked, biked, and dined with authors, lawyers, businesswomen, surgeons, entrepreneurs, behavioural therapists, dermatologists, computer scientists, artists, textile designers, psychologists, nutritionists, journalists, gemologists, and philanthropists, but never with a French hairstylist. Pascal spoke with a soft, sensual accent and mispronounced English in the most adorable way. He was fit, and small in stature. Sexy and boyish, and a big, big flirt.

We hiked the first few days together in a group. Then we began to hike apart from the others. We laughed and gossiped. We became instant friends. After four days of getting to know each other, Pascal felt comfortable enough to tell me what he had been holding back: that my hair was a hot mess. A disaster.

"Who cut your hair?" Pascal asked with disgust as he scoured my head. "It is not good. Your colour is too charcoal and the highlights too chunky and it doesn't match your own pigment and then you look green. You don't want to look green. You need more warm. Let me make you look beautiful. I have everything with me. Come to my room later and I will make you look sexy."

His sincerity and confidence, combined with the no-holds-barred surrender of my spa brain, propelled me without hesitation to say yes.

I tell you this because Pascal, a man I had known for

only four days, a man who could have been a serial killer, who could have cut my throat instead of cutting my hair, this heterosexual hairstyling stranger, I completely trusted. Alone in his phoneless, carbohydrate-free room, isolated at a spa in the middle of the California desert, I surrendered to the hands of Pascal Bensimon and was given the best haircut of my life. He coloured all fifty shades of grey with the artistry of Van Gogh and blew my hair out so full and sexy that Jennifer Lopez would have wept. From that moment on I became his groupie, a devoted fan, a crazy addict.

After my first haircut with Pascal, I trusted no one else to touch my hair. I know it seems preposterous that I couldn't find an equally good hairstylist in Manhattan, the mecca of sophistication and beauty, but I couldn't. Occasionally, however, when my work schedule prohibited me from making the twelve-hour commitment to Atlanta, I would be forced to go to a salon in New York. I'd book an appointment with some famous stylist to the stars who came highly recommended, and in good faith I would sit in his or her chair, wringing my hands incessantly and trying to conceal my increasing anxiety. None of the stylists, however, was as invested in the final result as Pascal was. They were indifferent and aloof. And I was intimidated. I would leave the salon enraged at the crazy cost and the inhumane treatment by the stupid Pink-wannabe technicians, and what's worse, the cookie-cutter matronly hairdo they'd give me. Most of the time, I'd leave looking like Leona Helmsley. I counted the days until I could fly back to Atlanta, where Pascal, my saviour, would restore my roots to their original colour and reinvigorate my confidence to the likes of Nicki Minaj.

My hair obsession was excessive, yes, but like an addict, I was unable to stop. I began to lie to my friends. I told them I was flying to Georgia for work, or visiting an old college roommate, or conducting a master class in acting at a local high school, or doing research at a restaurant chain because I was thinking of opening a raw food café.

Eventually, exhausted by my lies and running out of creative excuses, I came clean to a couple of friends. They were appalled. I think the word "insane" was bantered about. And then I became indignant.

"You know, it actually costs me less to fly to Atlanta than it does to get my hair cut at a fancy salon on Fifth Avenue," I argued. "And Pascal's cuts are consistent. And he's not condescending," I rationalized. "I mean, I am so sick of narcissistic assholes. They are defensive and they don't listen. They are so full of shit. And it's not as if I haven't tried," I pleaded.

I'd gone a few times to a fancy hair salon on Madison Avenue where the owner cuts everyone's hair from Hillary Clinton to Madonna—at least that's what he tells me. Anyway, I kept returning in spite of his cocky attitude because, miraculously, a few months ago he gave me a brilliant haircut.

"Oh my God, Jerome, I love what you've done," I said, stroking his already inflamed ego. "It's beautiful. And hip and youthful. Please do this every time."

Well, you'd think I'd insulted him. He moved on to his next client, some young movie star I was told, who I didn't recognize but he was all over, and without looking back at me he nodded his head dismissively and walked away.

The next appointment came, and I was giddy with anticipation. But after he finished with me, the haircut this time didn't at all look like the haircut he had given me months before. I said to him, hyperventilating but trying to hold it together, "Oh my gosh, Jerome, what did you do?" My speech was wavering, my voice uncomfortably high. "My hair is so uneven. My bangs are too short. And you covered all my highlights. I look like Judge Judy."

He replied defensively, "It's exactly what I did the last time. I didn't change a thing." With that, he vanished into his office with his little ugly pug dog and shut the door.

I was in shock. I sat for a few minutes looking at myself as I pulled my bangs down as far as the little severed hairs could travel.

Traumatized, I walked up to the receptionist and told her I was very unhappy with the way my hair turned out. I was near tears. I thought she would completely understand, being a woman with a head of hair herself, and not charge me. Instead, the Eva Braun of hair salons looked at me with a murderous glare and said, "That'll be $750 for today's services. Would you like to leave a tip?"

"Can you believe that?" I asked my friends. "They're all lying frauds and thieves, and I won't be caught dead in their salons. I'm not giving them a cent of my hard-earned money. Fuck them."

"My God, Andrea, you're completely out of control," they replied. "Listen to yourself. You're scary. That was just one salon. Certainly you can find someone here in New York that will do as good a job as the guy in Atlanta."

"It's my life. It's my hair, goddamnit," I shouted back defensively. I was rapidly turning into one of those frantic belligerent alcoholic mothers on *Intervention*, just before she's carted off to Betty Ford.

"My hair is important to me, don't you understand?" I yelled maniacally. "Jacques Lecoq taught us that *hair* is the most defining characteristic on a clown, I mean, a person." Now I was using my mime teacher to justify my uncontrollable hysteria. "And it's my livelihood, how I look," I continued, not even convincing myself with the obvious lie. No one to my knowledge had ever hired me, a sturdy character actress, because I was having a good hair day.

I was pacing and shouting and acting like a chicken with its coiffed head cut off.

"*Pascal is the only person who can make me look pretty, and no one can keep me from flying to Atlanta to get my hair cut!*"

After that outburst, we never talked about my hair again. My loving friends made a decision to treat my ongoing insane behaviour with compassion, as you would a mentally challenged child.

And so I kept making the twelve-hour trips to Atlanta, and never shared my secret with anyone else again.

2001

My dad and I were driving from Portsmouth, New Hampshire, back to Portland, Maine. We had been visiting my dad's first business partner and close friend, George Amergian.

Dad and I had been staying in Maine for a family reunion, and it had been my idea for us to make the drive together. Neither of us had seen George for a year, since he had been moved into a nursing home. I was now living in Toronto, and Dad had moved to Florida. Two years before, George had had a stroke and could no longer speak. But he was alert, understood everything, and had been so happy to see us. He was now in his eighties and understandably frail, the frailness that comes with immobility.

We had wheeled George around the nursing home, and I had tried my best to keep the mood upbeat, and Dad had tried his best to disguise his pain at feeling helpless. George would not be around for much longer, and Dad understood this would probably be the last time he would see his old friend. During our visit, Dad told and retold the same familiar stories that he and George had shared together. There was deep affection and tenderness between them. They laughed infectiously, these two proud Armenian men with a sixty-year history between them. They kept up the bravest of fronts for each other, even as it was time to say goodbye. They hugged and kissed. As George was wheeled down the long corridor and back to his room, Dad smiled and waved to his old friend for the last time.

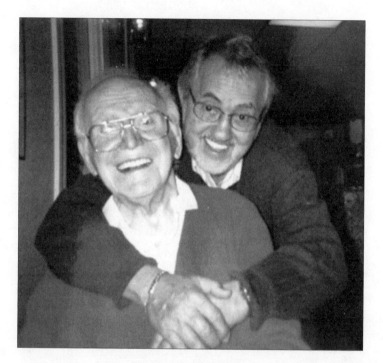

George (*left*), Dad (*right*)

Dad was silent as we got in the car. I felt the need, as I always did with my father, to keep talking.

I could not remember ever having an in-depth conversation with my dad. I had never been comfortable revealing how I really felt or who I really was for fear of being criticized. Our conversations were more like the superficial banter on a talk show. Dad was the host. He asked me light, trivial questions, and I, the perfect, good-humoured guest, answered him in a cheerful and non-confrontational manner. I made jokes and he laughed as if it were my job to entertain him. It kept us engaged but at a distance. I longed for an intimate connection. That's why I had suggested the trip. Dad was now in his eighties and I was in my fifties, and yet neither of us was at ease in each other's presence. This was going to be the perfect opportunity, I thought, for us to let down our guard and speak from our hearts. After all, we were in an enclosed vehicle, unable to run from each other even if the intimacy became unbearable.

Dad's demeanour was softer than usual. He was vulnerable after having spent time with his close friend. Our conversation began like it usually began. Dad asked me questions about my work, the same questions, the default questions, the safe questions, that he always asked.

"Do you have anything coming up, honey? Do you think you'll be working with anyone famous? Will it be better than the TV show you just did? I hope so. Jesus Christ, that was a terrible show. It wasn't very funny. None of my friends thought it was funny either. When do you think you'll get a break?"

I laughed loudly and uncomfortably.

"Well, Dad, I shot a movie a year ago, and it's out in theatres right now. It's called *Hedwig and the Angry Inch*. I don't think I've been more proud of anything. The movie has gotten rave reviews, and I've received some wonderful press from it. It's kind of an underground film but so cutting-edge and hip and smart, and John Cameron Mitchell is a genius, and I am honoured to be in his company. The music score is

brilliant, and I think it will win many awards. I would love
you to see it."

"I saw it," said my dad. "I didn't like it. I couldn't understand it. But your hair looked good."

This time I didn't laugh. I took a deep breath and held
on tightly to the steering wheel. When I regained my com-
posure, I spoke with compassion and clarity.

"Why would you say that, Daddy? Don't you know how
badly that makes me feel, how hurtful that is?" My dad was
silent.

"What did you think of my acting?" I continued. "All the
years you have seen me in plays and on TV and in movies,
you have never commented on my acting. You talk about the
other actors and how someone else stole the show, but with
me you only talk about how I look. It makes me feel like you
don't think I have talent. That you don't think I'm a good
actress. That someone else is always better. You have never
once told me you thought I was good in anything."

Dad lowered his head and stared at his feet. After a few
moments he spoke. His speech was halting and uncertain.
His voice cracked. He was crying.

"I don't know anything about acting," he tried to explain.
"But I do know about hair. I know what looks pretty."

My dad's vulnerability was heartbreaking. In that moment,
he was a child who had been caught and scolded and was
ashamed of what he had done. I was sorry I had confronted
him. I wanted to retract everything I had said.

Neither of us spoke. I kept driving. Dad wiped his eyes as he turned away and looked out the window.

I took his hand and held it. "Daddy, can we make a pact?"

"What is it, Andrea?" he asked quietly.

"From here on in, every time you see me in anything, whether you don't care for it or understand it," I said smiling reassuringly, "can you just say to me, 'Andrea, you were wonderful? I loved seeing you up there.' Can you do that?"

"Yes," said my dad as he continued to look out the window. "From now on, I'll never say anything else about your hair."

Dad kept his word. He never criticized a performance of mine again, nor did he ever mention my hair. From 2001 until he died in 2009 at the age of ninety-two, whenever he saw me in anything, he would say simply, like an obedient child, "You were wonderful. I loved seeing you up there."

2013

"Your dad loved you, Andrea," Paul Trusciani explained. "He probably said the things he said because he wanted to help you."

I was in Maine. I was staying at the Black Point Inn. I had come here to talk with Mr. Trusciani, now eighty and a long-time business associate of and best friend to my dad. I needed him to fill in the blanks so I could finish this story. I had been working on it for months and couldn't find an ending. I was hoping Paul had some answers.

I met him at his grocery store, Paul's, on Congress Street in downtown Portland. The space in which his grocery store stands has been the home to other grocers since 1900. All the years I lived in Portland, I'd walk by the store and never notice it. I was shocked at how absent I was in my youth.

"Your dad wanted to be successful. And he was. He was legendary. He had an eighth-grade education but was a marketing and retailing genius. He was my mentor. If it wasn't for him, I wouldn't have this supermarket. I loved your dad. Everyone did."

"Was he a perfectionist? Was he critical of the people who worked for him?" I asked.

Paul laughed. "Johnny used to say, there are two kinds of luck in the world. Good luck and bad luck. And the harder you work, the luckier you get. He hated it when people would tell him how much they liked his stores and restaurants. 'You can't learn from that, Paul,' he'd say. And so, with his employees, he wouldn't tell them what they did right, he would tell them what they did wrong. Then they could fix it and make it better. Bob Cott, who handled John's advertising, told me that John was probably the most conscientious, customer-driven client he had ever worked for. Your dad actually read each and every customer card. He expected absolute perfection from every one of his employees."

"But, Paul, that kind of pressure to be perfect is hard on a child. The message when I was growing up was that I was never good enough, that I never looked good enough."

"Your father was tough on women, tough on your mother. Appearances were important to him."

Paul laughed as he remembered an incident where my mom came into my dad's office and said she had just been to Weight Watchers and had lost six pounds. "She was so excited," Paul explained. "Your father looked at her and said under his breath, 'Look behind you, Sybil, and you'll find them.'

"He was hard on Liza too [my dad's second wife], always on her for what she ate and how she looked. He kept after his women. Listen, your father believed in persistence and determination. He wanted to help people succeed. And he wanted to help you. I bet he thought if you changed your hair, you would look like a Hollywood actress. Your dad loved beautiful women. He loved movie stars. He couldn't tell you how great you were because then he wasn't helping you, but if he could tell you how to look or wear your hair, like the Hollywood stars he saw in the movies, he could help you be as successful as they were."

"You know what my father asked me after I won my first Tony Award? He said, 'Now do you think you'll get a break?' It was preposterous, Paul. A Tony Award is the highest honour in the theatre."

"Listen, Andrea, all I can say is that your father was very proud of you. But he was never satisfied with what he had. He pushed himself. And he pushed you. He probably was hoping you'd be cast in a movie and become a big star like Lana Turner or Elizabeth Taylor or Gina Lollobrigida. That's what he meant by a break. You would be in something that everyone would see and then you'd be famous.

"I want to show you something."

Paul led me to the front of his grocery store. By the entrance, nailed to the wall, was a framed yellow paper with words written in calligraphy. I recognized the script. Dad was an unschooled yet talented graphic artist. He created all the print ads for his stores and restaurants.

"Your dad had this hanging on the wall in his office in the first supermarket he owned. He was only in his twenties when he opened that store. When he retired, I brought it to my store. It's been hanging on my wall for over twenty-five years. It's by Calvin Coolidge. Your dad lived by these words."

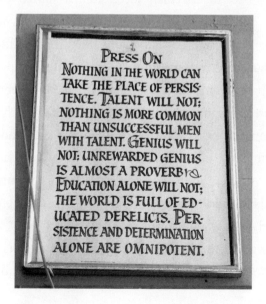

"Your dad was relentless at following through. He worked seven days a week. He always said that if the boss wasn't in the store, the store wouldn't survive. He deserved every nickel he ever made. He was generous to everyone. He was loyal. He expected the best. He worked hard, gambled hard, and loved to entertain. I remember him saying, 'Paul, if I die and I have $2 left, I'm gonna get up on the casket and spend it.'

"Your father was the best businessman I ever knew. Do you know that when he sold his six supermarkets, Martin's Foods, to Hannaford Brothers in 1972, he was in his fifties? He had already made millions of dollars in the supermarket business. He then opened The Art Gallery restaurant in downtown Portland, and the Merry Manor in Westbrook. And they became extremely successful. He started a second career in his fifties, and by the time he retired he owned and operated five restaurants in Maine, New Hampshire, and Massachusetts. It was just him. No committee, no partners, no company behind him. Just John Martin. He never looked back. Just kept moving forward, always thinking of the store, the restaurant, never John Martin. He was kind and had a wonderful sense of humour, and he was always watching out for his customers. John always delivered on his promises."

I told Paul about the trip in the car with my dad and how Dad had cried when I confronted him.

"You got through to him. He knew he was being too tough. Your dad had a good heart. Don't forget, Andrea, he was the son of immigrant parents who both died by the time he was thirteen. John wanted you to succeed. He loved his family. I'm not saying he would have been easy to live with. I'm not saying that appearances weren't important to him. But he loved you."

Paul and I walked across Congress Street to Starbucks, ordered coffee, and continued talking. It had been almost four hours since we began our conversation. That morning I had learned more about my dad's success as a businessman than I'd ever known growing up. But I was still searching for something. Yes, I had gained insight into our relationship, and an explanation for my crazy hair obsession. But I had expected the revelations to be emotionally cathartic. They weren't. In fact, I felt strangely detached.

I knew my dad had loved me. But what I came to realize, while writing this story, was that his love and criticism for me were inextricable. They were intertwined. Once the criticism had stopped, I felt a strange void. Without his criticism, his love felt empty. He was a brilliant businessman and innovator. He did the best he could as a father. He was generous and provided financially for his family—my brother and my sister and our children. He was a leader in his community. He was loved and respected among his peers. He was a good man, and I was proud of all he accomplished and proud to be his daughter. I loved him and laughed with him and to this day miss him dearly, but I finally understood that what I had been searching for, my dad was incapable of giving.

I longed to hear, as any child does, *You're perfect just the way you are*. But for my dad, perfection got you nowhere. Imperfection is what pushed you to success. It's what made you who you were.

I handed Pascal a page I had ripped out of a magazine showing a twenty-five-year-old model with platinum blonde hair.

"Do you like this, Pascal?" I asked. "I don't like my hair. I want to do something different." Two weeks earlier I had turned sixty-five.

Pascal glanced at the photo.

"*Mais oui*, every haircut looks better blonde. It will not look good on you. Now go get changed. I'm going to fix your hair. I'm going to make you younger. I'm going to make the colour right for you. Trust me and forget about everything. You are going to feel much better after my work. It is your birthday is why you feel that way. Is why everything bothers you. Every time you get a birthday, you feel fat and ugly. Everybody does."

"Do you think I'm crazy to fly to Atlanta to get my hair cut, Pascal?

"*Mais non*. You're lovely and we take care of you. And it's an investment on your beauty."

"Why do you think women come from all over the world to see you, Pascal?"

"Because I do something with love and passion that nobody else does."

"You certainly do, my darling. There's no one like you."

"And I adore women," he continued.

After Pascal cut and coloured my hair, he held up a mirror for me to peruse his handiwork.

"It looks beautiful," I said.

"*You* look beautiful," he replied as he gently and erotically brushed the little pieces of hair off my neck and back.

"Oh, Pascal," I said coyly. "You are bad. You are such a flirt. See you in eight weeks."

"*Oui, ma chérie. Au revoir.*"

As I was boarding the flight to New York that night I called a friend and asked if she wanted to have dinner when I got back to the city.

"Where are you?" she asked.

"I'm in Atlanta," I said unapologetically. "I just got my hair done and it looks fabulous."

"Atlanta?" she asked, surprised.

"Yup, Atlanta. Flew here this morning. I know it's crazy." I was laughing now. "But that's the way it is. That's who I am. I fly to Atlanta to get my hair cut."

"Well, I can't wait to see the new you."

"Fabulous," I said. "And I can't wait to show you."

Mommy

Christmas Eve, 1959

"'Have yourself a merry little Christmas, Let your heart be light . . .'"

Mommy is singing. She is getting dressed for a party she is about to throw for twenty guests. We are in her bedroom. She wears only pantyhose and high heels as she wiggles around her room. I am lying on her bed, watching her. I'm twelve.

"Andrea, pass me my bra, sweetheart."

She continues singing.

"'From now on, our troubles will be out of sight . . .'"

Mommy studies herself in the full-length mirror.

"My breasts look great," she says. "They are definitely my best feature."

I feel shy. Something about watching my mother parade around topless feels inappropriate, and yet I can't keep my eyes off her body. I ask my mom a question, but she doesn't respond. She's busy looking at herself. She turns sideways and holds in her stomach.

"Sybil Martin," she says out loud, "you are one classy lady."

"Mommy, can I ask you something? Mommy, are you listening?"

"Honey, go fix me another drink, and we'll talk about anything you want. V.O. Manhattan in a snifter, shaken not stirred. Oh, what am I saying, you know how to make it. Hurry, the party starts at seven."

My mother would have been eighty-five years old today if she had lived past her seventieth birthday. My mother died from a very painful lung cancer in January 1993. I'm not sure to this day that I mourned her death properly. I have an idea of how children should behave when one of their parents dies. And my behaviour was nowhere near what my expectations were. I have learned since my mom's death that everyone mourns differently, and that there should be no judgment on the way someone mourns. But I still can't forgive myself. I still feel I have done something wrong.

* * *

"What is the matter with you, Andrea, curled up in a ball? You're a moody one. Life is too short to spend feeling sorry for yourself. What did you want to ask me?"

"Nothing, Mommy."

I hear the doorbell ring. Oh no, the guests are starting to arrive.

"Andrea, honey, can you answer the door? Show them to the bar, and bring me my drink. Your mother's going to make an entrance tonight. We don't live in a two-storey house with a winding staircase for nothing."

My mom's name was Sybil. Sybil Angel Manougian. Isn't that exotic? Just like my mother. She was born to Angel Stepanian and Arax Manougian in Portland, Maine, in 1922. She grew up with three brothers and one sister in poverty in a three-room flat in the immigrant sec- 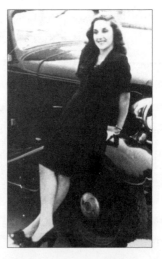 tion of downtown Portland. The children shared one bed, the house was seldom heated, and rats lived in the walls. Sybil and her sister, Dorothy, had the daily task of walking to the corner bakery, where, with a few pennies, they bought day-old bread for the family. Arax, their father, was born a Christian Armenian in Van, Turkey. In 1918, fleeing persecution and massacre, he left his homeland and arrived in Portland. He could not support his family with the few dollars he received each week as a neighbourhood barber, and his growing alcoholism eventually prevented him from providing for them at all. Angel, his wife, who was fifteen when Arax sent for her from Armenia to marry him, was a child herself, spoke no English, and had no knowledge as to how to raise five children on her own. When my mom was seventeen, she met my dad, John Papazian Martin, who was seven years her senior.

She quit high school at the insistence of her father, who believed that my dad would provide for her and rescue her from a life of poverty. My dad and mom got married in

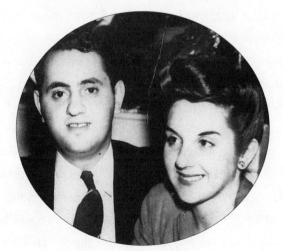

1944, at the height of the Second World War. They moved to Springfield, Massachusetts, where he was stationed with the air force. My mom was lonely and isolated, miles away from her family and friends. Her dreams of being a singer and living a creative life were no longer a reality. Her job now was to be a good wife.

Mommy is trying on many outfits for the party. She takes out a turquoise kimono and holds it in front of her.

"Look at this. The drycleaners shrunk it. They may adore me like all my homosexual friends do, but they don't know how to run a business. They should go back to hairdressing, where everyone was happy. Now go get ready."

"I am ready," I say.

"What do you mean, that's what you're wearing? You look like a waif. Okay, you know what? I'm too old to argue. It's your body. You have to live with it."

She picks out a pretty black sparkly sweater and a black sparkly skirt to wear. "Zip me up, sweetheart."

"Mommy, can I stay at Daddy's tonight? I don't want to go to the party."

"No, you are not going out on Christmas Eve with your father and that woman. You will see him tomorrow. As long as we are both alive, your father will come here every holiday and carve the family turkey. We may not be together, but he's the best thing that ever happened to this family. He's not good enough for me, but he's still your father."

Mommy hands me her lipstick, then continues singing.
"'Christmas comes but once a year.'"
"Come over here, Andrea. Help Mommy with her makeup
and we'll practise our duet."

My grandfather was correct: my dad did provide for my mom. After the war, they settled back again in Portland. By then my dad had worked his way up from being a stock boy in a grocery store to owning one. I don't think my mom and dad were ever in love. He was both charmed and annoyed at her vivaciousness and flair, and at the same time took great satisfaction in providing for her. My mom had enormous respect for my dad's business savvy but felt constrained in her role as a housewife. In 1947, I was born. My mom was twenty-four years old. My sister, Marcia, was born two and half years later, and eight years after Marcia, my brother, Peter, was born.

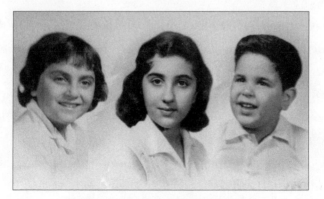

Marcia (*left*), me (*centre*), Peter (*right*)

My dad's businesses were flourishing—now three grocery stores and a restaurant—but my mom felt increasingly trapped. She wanted to work. He didn't want her to be away from the house and the family. Eventually, she convinced him to allow her to take art classes. A few years later, she became instrumental in nurturing and developing the careers of many young artists in Maine. She named one of my dad's restaurants, The Art Gallery, and hung paintings by emerging Maine artists on every wall. She was responsible for the sale of hundreds of paintings, though she never received an agent's commission. She was proud of her accomplishments and soon became a respected and beloved figure in Maine's art community. When I was twelve, my parents separated, but they were never legally divorced. After my mom's death, my dad would remarry, but while my mom was alive, my dad and she remained a constant presence in each other's lives.

"Look at you, Andrea. You're Mommy's little doll. The little doll I never had growing up. And then I had you. My own real dolly. I used to dress you like a little princess. I'd iron your little socks, and your ribbons, and your underpants. Then I'd put you in a carriage and show you off to all the neighbours, and if they wanted to touch you, I'd say, 'No, get away, that's my doll.'"

I like it when my mommy tells me stories about when I was a little girl. I wish she would keep talking, but she stops.

"Okay, you know what? I don't have time to be sad. Being

depressed is not at all becoming for a Martin. It's Christmas Eve. People are counting on us to be the life of the party. Jesus died for our sins; it's the least we can do."

My mother *was* the life of the party. She was the original Auntie Mame. Everyone loved being around her. She would hold court, captivating her audience with a great story in her dramatically raspy voice, then laughing infectiously. She loved to entertain. My friends adored her. My husband adored her. My kids adored her. She was a true original, a life force, uninhibited, gregarious, flirtatious, and fun. "Bob," she would say, looking up at my husband as she sat perched in her favourite chair, "hand me my crossword puzzle and my drink and come over here."

"Yes, Sybil."

"I love you, you know that, but our Andrea, she doesn't know how to treat a man."

Mom would never back down from a heated conversation. Her word was the last one. Dynamic, she oozed personality, like a movie star from the '40s. She was Bette Davis, traipsing around the room, delivering a soliloquy, gesticulating with one hand and holding a Manhattan in the other.

We were at a family dinner party at Marty and Nancy Short's home in the late '80s. Marty's sister, Nora, was there with her husband, Ralph, who was reserved and introverted. Nora and my mom were like two peas in a pod, outgoing and loud, and they loved their cocktails. They had been laughing together for hours. Mom stood up in the middle of the dinner and made a toast. "To Nora, my friend," she said, holding up her glass and sounding like Gloria Swanson in *Sunset Boulevard*. "Nora, darling, we have *got* to find you a man." She then sat down, continued pontificating, and was oblivious to the rest of the table's stunned silence.

"Go put on your prettiest party dress for Mommy and a great big smile. Smile. I know there's a smile. I love you. Listen, sweetheart, tonight it would really mean a lot to Mommy if you didn't call her Mommy. Call me Sybil. Okay? Especially in front of the general. Let me hear you say it. 'Sybil.'"
"Sybil."
"That's right. I love you. How do I look?"
"Pretty, Mommy."
"Well, then, let us go."

Mom was visiting me and my sons in Pacific Palisades in 1992. She was noticeably tired, resting more than usual and staying in bed past her standard 6 a.m. wake-up, when the typical routine would have been to put on her exercise clothes, sip a cup of strong black coffee, and do sit-ups and leg raises in her room. She no longer had interest in cooking for us, something she had always taken great pride in. With her endless energy, she had always been able to outrun her grandsons, but now instead she slept on the couch for hours every day. She returned to Portland, where her doctor delivered the devastating news. She had lung cancer and a year to live. She was sixty-nine years old. She had not smoked for over forty years and was a specimen of good health.

Over the next year, I travelled often from Los Angeles to Maine to be with my mom. I read books by Ram Dass, Stephen Levine, and Elisabeth Kübler-Ross as I tried to make peace with this incomprehensible disease. I joined a meditation group. I took massage classes so I could learn how to touch her and alleviate some of her pain. I knit blankets for her, socks for her, anything I could to comfort my mother.

Mom was very sick with only a few weeks to live the last time I visited her. She was in agony from the cancer, which had spread to the lining of the pleura. Every breath she took was torture. She had a morphine drip implanted and a nurse stayed with her round the clock.

We were in her bedroom. She was sitting in a chair and I was sitting on the floor by her side. "Mommy, would you like me to massage your feet?" I asked.

"If it will make you feel happy, Andrea." Mom, smiling, could barely get the words out.

I put some baby oil in my hands and began to massage my mom's feet. "Let me do this for you, Mommy. I know I can make you feel better. How does this feel?"

"If it makes you feel good, Andrea, that makes me happy."

"Would you like me to read to you, Mommy?" My mom's eyes were closed, but she nodded her head yes.

I began.

"Let yourself open to receive the moment, as it is in mercy and loving kindness."

Mom lets me read to her, but I know she's not really listening. She's in and out of consciousness. "Mom, I'm so sorry for your suffering. I can read more to you, Mommy, if you like."

"Go ahead, honey, if it makes you feel good. I love comforting you."

I don't remember ever seeing my mom without makeup on. She always looked her best, and loved to look pretty, like the little dolls she never had. As she lay in her bed now, her usually dyed-black hair was sparse and grey, but she had managed to do her face. She wore shimmering green eye shadow, mascara, and the same vibrant coral lipstick she had used for years. She wanted to look "done" when the doctor came to visit.

She opened her eyes and stared at me. She spoke in a whisper. Breathing was unbearable. Even the morphine drip could not dull her pain, nor could it dull the reality of her imminent death.

"Why me, Andrea? Why me?"

"I'm so sorry, Mommy. I wish I could do something to take away your pain."

"I know, honey. I need to sleep now. I'm tired."

* * *

My mother died a week later, the day after I flew back to Los Angeles. When I got home, I tried to write a scene for my one-woman show about my mom and me. It took months and a nervous breakdown to get up enough courage to write about a woman with whom I had unresolved conflict but whom I loved deeply.

It seems preposterous that a woman with so much vitality is no longer alive. I am so sad that my sons missed out on knowing their grandmother as they grew older. They would have worshipped one another. She would have taken them around the world, brought them to the opera, to the theatre, to concerts, and enriched their lives with her unbridled passion for living. She would have pushed them to reach for the stars.

"Jack and Joe, come in here," she'd be saying. "Let's practise some Christmas songs before everyone arrives. Do you know 'Have Yourself a Merry Little Christmas'? It's my favourite."

"No, Nanny," my boys would say. "How does it go?"

"'Through the years we all will be together, if the fates allow . . .'" Nanny would start to sing.

Jack would get behind the piano, and Joe would get out his sax, and Nanny would continue, a drink in her hand, beaming proudly at her two grandsons, and they'd accompany her, and finally guests would arrive and join in, and the atmosphere would be jolly and festive, and the fire would be roaring, and snow outside the window would be falling, and my mom, their nanny, would make that moment into the best goddamn party there ever was.

"Hang a shining star upon the highest bough,
And have yourself a merry little Christmas, now."

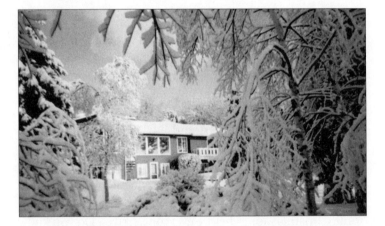

Mom's house, Cumberland Foreside, Maine

Secrets

I guess you could call it a nervous breakdown. No one ever used that word to describe my condition. But that's what it felt like to me.

In February 1993, a month after my mom died and a year after losing my best friend to AIDS, I fell apart. My bulimia was at its height. I was divorced, living in Pacific Palisades, California. I was isolated and unemployed, and trying to be a mom to my two young sons, who were nine and eleven. I was crippled by depression. My first waking moments began with a glimmer of hope. Please God, I would pray, please let this new day bring me peace. Please help me be a good mother. With the little bit of energy I had, I would struggle to make the boys breakfast, help them get dressed, and drive them to school. I would try desperately to listen to them as they shared what was going on their lives—homework, music lessons, sports, sleepovers. I couldn't hear them. I wasn't present for them. I was consumed with fear. I felt like a failure. My sons were my world, but even they could not compete with the hostile punishing voices in my head. All I wanted was to be alone, with food, in my bed, escaping the reality of my life.

After I dropped them off at school, I'd get back in the car and be crippled with self-doubt. Where should I go? Who could I talk to? Should I start the car and keep driving? Should I call their dad and tell him to take the boys, confess to him that I didn't think I was capable of raising our sons, that I was a terrible mother, that I was riddled with anxiety and my panic attacks were out of control? The only thing that calmed the anxiety was driving to Gelson's supermarket, where I would buy wine, cookies, ice cream, cake, loaves of bread, cheese, and candy. I would drive back to my home, where I would binge on everything I could swallow and keep down, and then I'd make myself throw up and binge some more.

I told no one about the black hole I lived in. I believed that I'd be all right if only I could control my bingeing and purging. I would go back to bed until it was three o'clock and time to pick up my sons. Again I would attempt a cheerful demeanour as I pretended to listen.

From the time I got back home with them at four, I would stare at the clock and pray for night—two hours, two minutes, one minute before I could put my sons to bed, and then I would binge all over again. If I didn't have food in the house, I would leave my sons alone, while they slept, and would drive in desperation to the store, binge in the car, and then drive home recklessly to purge again. I'd binge until I couldn't feel. Every night I would fall asleep with a distended stomach, a burning swollen throat, and the smell of vomit on my fingers. And then one morning, I broke. I had finally come apart. I called the boys' dad, hysterical and unable to breathe, and told him to pick up the boys. Then I called the nearest hospital.

I don't remember the details of how I found the psychiatric ward at Centinela Hospital in Inglewood. All I remember is some intake person over the phone asking about insurance and me responding with "Call my business manager," but mostly I was crying, begging them to help me: "I can't stop bingeing and purging and I'm scared I'm not going to make it and I don't know what to do and I need someone to talk to, somewhere to go that's safe. Please help me. I don't know how to be a mother. I can't be alone with my children. Please, I can't do this anymore."

I checked into the eating disorders unit at Centinela and stayed for a month. I was one of eight female patients. Our eating disorders ranged from bulimia and anorexia nervosa to obesity. All of our eating disorders were accompanied by depression, despair, denial, rage, and shame. We were medicated with antidepressants and monitored by a psychiatrist who visited twice a week.

The youngest patient was fifteen and anorexic. She weighed sixty-five pounds. This was the third rehab her parents had sent her to. She was defiant and didn't believe she belonged there. Every day she begged to leave. She had outbursts constantly and was disruptive.

The oldest woman was in her fifties, five feet tall, and weighed over three hundred pounds. She had four children. She was unemployed, on disability, and divorced. Her children had been taken away from her. She didn't know how to stop eating. She was not functioning. She was severely depressed. She wanted her children back.

There was a beautiful young girl in her early twenties who was addicted to crystal meth. She had started taking it a few years earlier to lose weight and then got hooked. She did not think she had a problem. She said she could stop anytime but that she liked the feeling of being high. She was in sales, a good-paying job, and had been given an ultimatum. That was the only reason she was there.

We had group therapy every day, where we sat in a circle with our facilitator, who was a recovering anorexic, and we talked about our lives and our addictions and what events had brought us to the hospital. We had art therapy classes, where we had to draw what we thought we looked like. I drew a circle for my head but couldn't draw in my face. I had no conception of what I looked like. I had always adapted to what other people wanted me to be. Without their input, my face was a blank canvas.

We had to learn to eat differently. We had to eat slowly and talk about what feelings came up as we ate. I had never thought about how food tasted before. Food was my drug of choice. I had been bulimic for almost fifteen years. I consumed food quickly so as to not feel. I didn't care if I stole half-eaten food off someone's room-service tray that lay in the hotel hallway or picked garbage out of a wastebasket after throwing it out. I would eat at the fanciest, most expensive restaurants with a group of friends, then excuse myself, go to the washroom, throw up, return to the table, and eat again. Not feeling was the only purpose food ever held for me.

I had been obsessed with my weight all my life. I had been chubby as a child but never obese, and yet at age thirteen I was prescribed my first diet pills. Eskatrol, they were called. Little orange pills. Basically, the pills were speed. I took diet pills all through high school. When the doctor would no longer prescribe them, I started exercising compulsively.

It was in my late twenties that I discovered bulimia as a way to control my weight. I was living in Toronto and appearing in the Second City stage show. Our group had replaced the original members, three of whom had left after being cast in *Saturday Night Live*—Gilda Radner, Dan Aykroyd, Bill Murray. We were at a reunion party with the original cast. Gilda was clearly the breakout star on *SNL*. Every so often as we talked at the party, she would excuse herself. I asked her where she was going and she said to the bathroom, where she was making herself throw up. It was a way to control her weight, she said. And she wanted to keep slim with all the attention she was now getting on *SNL*. I thought at that moment, *If Gilda's doing it, then so will I.* It seemed harmless to me. I don't think the disease even had a name, and if it did, I wasn't aware of it. No one in my circle talked about eating disorders. I rationalized my behaviour by saying I wasn't the only person to do this kind of thing. I reminded myself of the Romans and the way they ate: gorged, threw up, and gorged again. Throwing up as a way to look and feel good seemed glamorous.

Gilda wrote a book entitled *It's Always Something* in which she chronicles her battle with bulimia. I never confided in her that I picked up the practice. I wonder if we could have helped each other. Gilda died of ovarian cancer when she was forty-two. You would think that her tragic death would have stopped my destructive behaviour, but I continued, in silence, through both my pregnancies, and through my marriage.

My eating disorder was a secret that kept me sick for so long. It was not until I got into the hospital and heard like-minded people talk about their addictions that I got the courage to admit my addiction myself.

We were not allowed to exercise at the hospital. After the lights went out, I would lie on the hospital floor at the side of my bed and do sit-ups compulsively for hours. When we went for our afternoon walks as a group, we were not allowed to run or jog—anything that looked like exercise was forbidden. The nurses kept us in line. We were accompanied to our rooms after we ate, to keep us from throwing up. All packages of honey and sugar were rationed. Anything that we could binge on was taken away. We went on outings to restaurants to learn how and what to order and then how to eat what we ordered.

As I write this, I know that to the normal person it all seems crazy. But for those of us who had an unnatural relationship to food, the act of ordering and eating was fraught with profound anxiety. At our first outing to Baja Fresh, a fast-food chain that uses healthy and fresh ingredients, I stared for thirty minutes at the menu and, with my therapist by my side gently supporting me, tried to order. Every item on the menu was the enemy staring back at me, wanting to control and destroy me. It wanted to lodge in my stomach and make me fat and ugly and undesirable and alone and unsafe. I hated ordering. I hated eating what was placed in front of me. But I had no choice. And I wanted to get better. I knew I had hit bottom. I knew there was no place else for me to go. I had to face the feelings that came up while I had food in my stomach, and the feelings that came up when the meal was over. I was in my late forties. I had repressed many feelings. And mostly they started with shame.

My sister, Marcie, always jokes with me that we must have had different parents. We remember our childhood differently. I once asked Marcie if she ever woke up with anxiety.

She stared at me in disbelief and answered, "No, never. Why, do you?"

"Marcie," I replied, "there hasn't been a day in my life when I *haven't* woken up with anxiety. That's how I start my day. For the rest of my waking hours, I am feeding the tiger!"

For whatever reason—whether it was having a critical and controlling dad or a narcissistic mom, being the first-born, having an addictive personality, being overly sensitive, or having an unresolved karma from another life—from the moment I came out of my mom's womb, I needed more. Of everything. To fill me.

I chose food and then alcohol, and only when the unmanageability of my life became greater than the fear of letting the destructive behaviour go was I willing to change.

After I left the hospital, and after another month of outpatient care, I had more slips with my bulimia. But my stay in the hospital gave me the courage to continue on the path of recovery. I realized I wasn't going to die if I kept the food down, if I put on a few pounds, and slowly I stopped bingeing and purging. I have been in recovery from bulimia for twenty-one years now. And I haven't had a drink for twenty-two.

In all honesty, my obsession with my weight continues. It's still difficult for me to eat in a restaurant. I would prefer unwrapping a Lean Cuisine meal and putting it in the microwave to sitting down and talking with a group of people over dinner. I want to get the food thing out of the way so that I can be present for the company I'm with. But I no longer take pills, go on restrictive diets, or starve myself. I exercise moderately. If I have any feelings, happy or sad, my inclination is to stuff them down. But instead I sit with them. I feel what I'm feeling until it passes.

I am grateful to have hit bottom. I pray that my sons will understand after reading this why their mom was not always there for them while they were growing up. I have enormous guilt about the years I spent acting out and hiding. I know both my marriage and my children suffered from the result of my addictions. I hope my sons forgive me, though I know it may take a lifetime of uncovering and facing their own truth and pain. I want to believe I did the best I could, like my mom, who did the best she could. My grandmother survived a genocide, and when she died took many secrets with her. I hope I have been able to stop the cycle of secrets in my family. I want my boys to stand up proudly and own who they are, warts and all. Shame passed down through generations is palpable. Authenticity trumps all.

My intention in writing this is to speak the truth, and in so doing, give something back to my sons. Every day, I'm grateful for the opportunity to make up to them the years I took away.

Part Two

My Writing Process

Here's how I write. First, I obsess. Then, I eat. Then I comb the Internet for travel websites, news websites, and entertainment websites. Then I Google my own name. Disgusted with myself *and* my career, I call my agent for any work updates. If there aren't any, I'll randomly text messages and smiley faces to my friends. Or I'll search for more descriptive emoticons. Nothing like an animated lobster-claw emoticon to make a point.

Did you know that with a colon, a long dash, and a closing parenthesis you can text a face of a liar?

Long nose = liar. :———)

Or try texting a bunny.

```
(\_/)
(='.'=)
(")_(")
```

It's a more advanced emoticon, but so cute. You don't need an emoticon vocabulary to identify the bunny. It really looks like one. Emoticons can keep me occupied for hours.

I committed to writing a chapter this past week. I stared at the computer for two hours the first day I tried to write. I then called 3-1-1 to complain to the City of Toronto about algae on the pond in my backyard. I called Animal Control to complain about an unidentified animal nest in my eaves-trough. I ironed my sheets. I made two batches of whole-wheat bread from scratch. I sewed a button on my winter coat. But I didn't write. That was Sunday.

Monday I woke up and said to myself, *This is the day, Andrea. Today you are going to sit and write the chapter that you committed to writing.* I made coffee, cleaned off my desk. Positioned my chair so it was just the right height. Windexed my office window to let in more light, and opened a new docu-ment in Microsoft Word. I then went to the gym. I worked out for two hours, an hour more than I usually do, in order to stall the inevitability of staring again at the computer. I came back home, took a shower, put on my best writing wardrobe—loose jeans and crisp white shirt—woke up my computer, and took a nap. Monday. Another day of not writing.

It's Tuesday. Today is the day. I just got a text message from my friend Seth, the person to whom I had committed out loud that I was going to write. His text: "Where's your new chapter?"

I texted back a sad face. :-(and the words "Trying today."

He texted me: "I want it by late afternoon. Just write, even if it sucks."

"I know," I texted. "Why is it so effing hard? Nothing in my life is that blocked. Not even my rectum."

Another text from him: "Hilarious. First line of chapter."

"Too vulgar?" I ask.

"Funny," he responds.

"Would 'bowel' be better?" I ask.

He texts back: "Rectum."

So I am writing. When I commit out loud to something, I follow through. However, to continue with the rectum metaphor, I'm afraid that what I'm writing is shit.

Everyone tells you not to judge what you are writing. Let it flow out of you, don't go back and read what you write. So instead I finished that last sentence, walked away from the computer, and made myself an egg sandwich. I just returned to the computer, and *then* reread what I wrote.

I clicked on Word Count: 529 words. Is that enough for a chapter? Can I text my friend Seth a happy face? :-)

What about a really, really happy face? :-)) (Also known as a double chin in emoticon-speak.)

I'm going to take a nap (a really tired emoticon). **%-|**

Hmm. I wonder what a self-hating emoticon would look like? I'm going to research that. For three hours.

Then it's time for dinner. **<*{{{>< **(catch of the day).

Then bed. Then Wednesday. The day of the new chapter.

Here Are Some Other Things I'd Rather Do Than Write

Try on old dresses to see if they still fit
Get a manicure
Get a pedicure
Get a massage
Get a facial
Cut the grass
Water the lawn
Fill in the holes the raccoons dug up
Cut some hydrangeas
Dust my books
Do laundry
Wash dishes
Unloosen my belt
Return emails
Chat with telemarketers on the phone
Floss

Organize my playbills

~~Listen to my Josh Groban CD~~

See a movie

See an opera

String pearls

Make an origami hat

Listen to my fountain

Count my change

Pluck my chin hairs

Vacuum

Take a bath

Empty my wastebasket

Talk to strangers

Make lists

Make coffee

Make more coffee

Fluff pillows

Climb the Grand Canyon

Iron my sheets

Play with rats

Someday My Prince Will Come

t's Wednesday. The day of the new chapter. I just started a fire in the fireplace because I'm sure it will inspire me to write. Isn't that what happens in movies? Flames flicker as memories are unearthed; dreams, revealed; writer's block, unblocked. So romantic a notion, if you're Cate Blanchett.

All I want to do in front of the fire is sleep, or stare into space, or fluff pillows on my couch, or sweep up the embers that occasionally pop outside the fireplace screen, or fan the flames, or reposition the logs with my iron poker, or wipe down the mantel so it is free of soot, or eat a pound of 80 percent dark chocolate as the wood smoulders and the sparks fly. That's what a fire in the fireplace makes *me* want to do: clean, sleep, eat, organize. Here's what it doesn't make me want to do: *write*.

Shit, fuck, cock, pussy, dicklicker. Sure, judge me and my choice of words. And then *you* try to write a book. *I have nothing important to say.* That's the first thought that pops into my mind. Everyone has said whatever I want to say better than I could say it, even if they have never thought it. I'm a performer. I need an audience. In the moment, right here and right now. When I write a funny line, I want to hear applause. Without it, I am crippled. How can I write a book when each word I write I have to say out loud, pause, imagine a response, acknowledge the response in my mind, gesture to the imaginary audience with appreciation, and then write the next sentence? This book is going to take years. And I'm already a senior citizen.

I now understand the notion of a muse. All the great painters have had muses, nude ethereal models that have been the source of the artists' inspiration whenever they begin to doubt themselves. That's not the kind of muse I need—a penis hanging between the legs of a beautiful Abercrombie & Fitch boy will not motivate me to create. What I need is a laugh track piped into my office. Surround sound of whoops and cheers and cackles.

Years ago, in my twenties in Toronto, I volunteered to read books for the Canadian National Institute for the Blind. The book I was assigned was the weighty novel *The Brothers Karamazov.* I had to read for five hours at a time, in a small, windowless, soundproof room. There was a mic, a table, the book, and a chair. There was no interaction from any human being with the exception of a disembodied voice as I entered the room. "Andrea, we're recording," and then five hours later, the same disembodied voice, "Andrea, that's it for today." In between those two lines of communication was five hours of solitary confinement.

Here's what happened to me during the course of reading the six-hundred-page book. As soon as the door of the studio was closed shut and I found myself alone, staring at the print on the page, my entire upper lip slowly became numb. As soon as I started reading the first paragraph, I felt my upper lip falling asleep, as your arm does if you are lying on it for hours. Just dead weight. My lip dead weight as I pronounced all the Karamazov brothers' names. The good people at the Canadian National Institute for the Blind never commented on my sloppy articulation.

Fortunately, my upper-lip paralysis has never happened since. There's a reason for that. Now when I record anything, whether it be commercials, books on tape, or animation, there are glass windows in the studios, and I can see the bobbing head of the director or technician and these visible reactions are all I need to ensure that my upper lip stays mobile and lubed.

Here's why I believe I was stricken with an immovable upper lip when I read in that windowless, soundproof room, trying to bring the book and characters to life: there was no one cheering me on. I was alone, in my head, with no distractions. And that is not a pretty place to be. My mind, a gridlock of self-doubt, is so powerful that it anaesthetized the very tool I needed to create.

I am certain that my success as an improviser with Second City came from the fact that there was no time for second-guessing as I performed on stage. Thoughts and ideas came into my head, I said them, there was a reaction from the audience, and the audience's instant validation encouraged my free-floating spontaneity.

I have given real thought to the idea of hiring a young man who loves to laugh, who is a fan, who thinks I'm funny, and have him sit on my couch in my living room as I stand and pace improvising in the moment—delicious dialogue, hysterically funny and uninhibited ideas, free of self-doubt. He records my every word and then he transcribes what I say and, voilà, a book is written. I might do it. But now I'm alone in my office in my little home in Toronto. I see the occasional squirrel and the occasional duck outside my window. I wish they understood English. And were fans. Think of how much I would have written today. A menagerie of animals cheering me on. Wait, isn't that what kept Snow White working away as she waited for the Seven Dwarfs to come home for lunch? Skunks and birds and bunnies outside her kitchen window kept her company, encouraged her as she swept the floor in her cottage and sang in her sugary-sweet soprano. Her animal muses inspired her as she prepared stew for Dopey and Sleepy and Happy. They made her believe that her Prince Would Come.

Snow White didn't have alone time to second-guess. If she had given any thought about the trappings of her life, a confined life rivalled only by that of the seventy-eight wives of Warren Jeffs, she would have been out of there in a heartbeat. Her muses kept her focused on the task at hand. *How do I keep the Johnnie Walker away from Dopey?* she might have queried. Or, *What am I doing slaving away for seven irritating, overly sexed three-foot-tall men? Shouldn't I get overtime? And I wish everyone would stop calling me Snow White. I'm not so pure. I have really dark thoughts. For one, I hate Happy. Fuck Happy. No one can be that happy all the time. I am going to put rat poison in Happy's porridge and then there will only be six dwarfs and more room for me on the tiny fucking bed.*

But Stinky the Skunk and Binky the Bunny made sure that Snow White would not fall down the hellhole of despair. Stinky kept Snow White singing and sweeping and delighting in the fact that she was the matriarch in a home consisting of seven grateful misfits. And over the years, we have benefited from her muses. We have read her story and believe that our prince will come one day also. It took a village of animals and dwarfs to get Snow White's message across. An appreciative audience egging her on.

Now I feel better. I thought I was alone in my need to have a cheering section. I'm going to stop comparing myself to Margaret Atwood. She's an amazing writer, but I'm better on television. We all have unique gifts. And we all have to do whatever it takes to make them materialize.

I'm going to have a nap now, in front of the fire. But when I wake up, I'm calling this young kid I know, who in fact *looks* like an Abercrombie & Fitch model, and I'll pay him to strip and laugh as I dictate my book to him. I'm looking forward to completing a chapter and hearing my muse's laughter and staring for a long time at his penis. I'll do whatever it takes to complete this fucking book.

Television vs. Books

For years I said that I didn't watch television. And I didn't. I still say it. Only now I'm lying. I watch TV. A lot of TV. *Dr. Drew on Call, Antiques Roadshow, The Little Couple, The Amazing Race, Dancing with the Stars, So You Think You Can Dance, American Idol,* National Geographic Channel, Fireplace Channel, Cottage Life, and *Intervention,* the mother of all reality television. Any makeover show, especially if it involves surgery—better yet, stomach bypass surgery. I love before and after shots. I love to see a five-hundred-pound man after he has lost three hundred pounds and can fit into a size thirty-two pant; it brings me to tears. I'm applauding him as I sit in front of my television, devouring a pint of Ben & Jerry's Chocolate Fudge Brownie ice cream dripping with hot fudge sauce. I haven't picked up a book and been really enthralled since *The Girl with the Dragon Tattoo* and all the other escapades the tattooed girl experienced in the next two sequels. Occasionally, I'll pick up a magazine—*Time, Maclean's, Psychology Today*—read an article on Chinese counterfeit medicine, and feel like I have enough ammunition to carry on a ten-minute conversation with some knowledge that doesn't have anything to do with my career.

But I'd rather talk, and boy can I talk—about obsessive stage mothers from Arkansas, or the wonders of the career and marriage of a three-foot-tall little person, or how a crocodile can devour a wildebeest in twenty seconds or less. I sat glued to the television when a retired couple from Mississippi were told on *Antiques Roadshow* that an old iron poker they found in their attic was now worth $40,000. Come on, that is riveting entertainment and at the same time motivating. Who hasn't, after watching that show, cleaned out a closet in hopes of finding an unexpected windfall?

Am I illiterate? Will any book ever be able to hold my interest as much as Tom Sizemore getting sober on *Celebrity Rehab*? Have I destroyed my brain and its capacity to really expand and learn important things? I'm not selling out, am I? I will still camp out on Toronto mayor Rob Ford's front lawn if he brings up the ludicrous and decadent idea of closing libraries again. Does that make me a hypocrite? I love libraries. My best and most loyal friend, the library, since I was eight years old. How many hours would I spend in the Portland Public Library when I was a child? A recluse among Longfellow and Robert Louis Stevenson, Emerson and Thoreau. If they lived in Maine, or even passed through the state, I was captivated with what they had to say.

"'Between the dark and the daylight, When the night is beginning to lower, Comes a pause in the day's occupation, That is known as the Children's Hour' . . . 'Listen my children, and you shall hear, Of the midnight ride of Paul Revere.'"

The Runnymede Public Library was a home for me and my two small children at least four afternoons a week when I was a young mom. The storytelling hours and the dedicated teacher-librarians created a magical world for every kid sitting cross-legged on the floor. *The Very Hungry Caterpillar, The Giving Tree, Are You My Mother?, Jacob Two-Two, Alligator Pie.* Those books and the little room upstairs

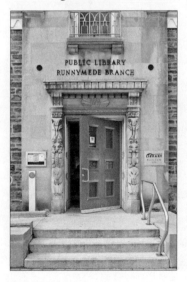

that housed them was a second home for us. It kept me from feeling isolated and made me feel like a "good mom" 'cause I was introducing my kids to books.

The library opened at ten. On the way there, we strolled through High Park and talked about nature and why Canada geese fly south in the winter. In those days,

I knew the answer. Or if I didn't, we'd find the answer in a book, together.

Now that part of my inquisitive, literate brain has stopped working.

Instead, I make myself a cup of tea, turn on the TV, and check out. Maybe that's the question. Not if TV is bad and books are better. Maybe the question is why do I feel the need to check out? And why can't books help me do that? It takes a lot of brain power with no distractions to read a book. Now, if I could board a plane and travel to the moon, I could get through every book in my library.

These are the books that sit on my night table, patiently waiting to be picked up and read: *The Goldfinch*, *Wise Children*, *The Great Gatsby*, *Bring Up the Bodies*, *How I Became a Famous Novelist*. I climb into bed, stare at the books, and shame myself to sleep. Too many thoughts of the day, my life, my kids' lives, my career, the environment, politics, unemployment, foreclosures, sadness, hopelessness, injustice, despair. *No* book can distract me from all that.

Wait, that's a lot of responsibility to put on a little book. I think I'm looking at this reading thing the wrong way.

Instead of needing to be distracted, maybe I could let myself be inspired. Elevated. Transported. Instead of thinking about what a book can't do, let me think about what it can do.

That's it. I'm going to march into my bedroom right now, and pick up *The Goldfinch*, and pour myself a cup of tea, and get all cozy in my down-filled chair, and put my feet up on the ottoman, and start reading. I'm so excited. Wait, what time is it? 7:45 p.m. Perfect. I have fifteen more minutes to read before I have to stop. It's elimination round on *American Idol* tonight. I'm psyched to see what JLo is wearing and to hear what my lover, Keith Urban, will say. Every word that comes out of his sumptuous and sultry Australian mouth keeps my lady parts* all aflutter. I'd like to put a steak on *his* barbie.

*Book title alert.

Chimps in Tutus

Growing up in the '50s and '60s, I watched a lot of television variety shows. Jackie Gleason, Ernie Kovacs, Sid Caesar's *Your Show of Shows*, Carol Burnett. Those programs, and the comedians on them, gave me a sense of belonging. I remember thinking that if those people could be up there making faces, then maybe there was a place for me. Twenty years later, I found a home on *SCTV*, a Canadian variety/sketch show, where for seven years I got to make my own funny faces.

The variety show was at one time the most popular form of entertainment. It all started with vaudeville. Eventually, vaudeville led to Sid Caesar and Imogene Coca, and the ultimate variety show of its time, *The Ed Sullivan Show*. Who remembers Ed Sullivan? It's hard to explain Ed Sullivan today. He wasn't funny; he didn't sing or dance or do impressions, though he was often imitated. He had no discernible talent and appeared uncomfortable. I grew up with Ed Sullivan and remember all the acts: musicians, dance duos, comedians, magicians, acrobats, jugglers, male and female impersonators, and trained animals. Topo Gigio, the little Italian mouse ("Hello, Eddie! Hello, Eddie!") maybe the first openly gay rodent on network television, and Señor Wences, the Spanish ventriloquist. He would hold a box with a talking head in it and ask the box, "Are you all right?" Then he'd open the box and the head would say, "All right." This would entertain me for hours. It was such an innocent time.

I had two favourite acts on *The Ed Sullivan Show*. One was the Marquis Chimps. One Sunday night, the Marquis Chimps were doing a seven-minute routine involving five chimpanzees dressed in tuxedoes, prom dresses, and tutus. Riding tricycles, jumping on trampolines, turning somersaults, flying by on roller skates, playing drums, dancing the twist, you name it. The show was running long one night, so the stage manager goes up to the trainer, Mr. Marquis, and says, "Ya gotta cut three minutes." Mr. Marquis says, "I can't." The stage manager asks, "Why not?" Mr. Marquis says, "These are chimpanzees, not teamsters. They've rehearsed a seven-minute routine, and that's what they're gonna do. I'll tell you what we can do. We can start the act behind the curtain, and three minutes in, just bring the curtain up. That's the best I can do." The stage manager says, "Great." So for three minutes, behind the curtain like some long-lost Samuel

Beckett play, a group of multi-talented monkeys performed their hearts out for no one. Three minutes in, the curtain goes up to tumultuous applause, with the chimps already in progress. Today, we couldn't have an act like that on TV. Someone would call it cruelty to animals. Those chimps knew their place. Mr. Marquis would put a banana on one of the chimps' foreheads and the chimp would sit there for five minutes staring out, not touching the banana until Mr. Marquis said he could eat it. Where was Mr. Marquis when I was bringing up my kids?

My other favourite involves Clyde Beatty, the famous lion tamer who did what was known as a "fighting act." Mr. Beatty would walk into a cage filled with lions, tigers, cougars, and hyenas, with a whip and a pistol strapped to his side. This one night on the Sullivan show, he walks into the cage, and he's cracking the whip and yelling at these creatures, and, well, nobody likes that kind of behaviour, especially wild animals being forced to perform on television, and the lions and tigers in essence called a wildcat strike and turned on Beatty. Suddenly, the camera cuts to Ed, not exactly a brilliant improviser, who says nervously, "Let's see who we have in the audience tonight." Meanwhile, in the background you hear Clyde Beatty firing shots and screaming, "Open the door, for Chrissake, open the goddamn door!" More growling, gun shots, and laughter from the hyenas. By this time Ed is in the audience interviewing, of all people, Carol Channing, who is currently starring in *Hello, Dolly!*

Ed says, "Well, look who's here, it's Carol Channing, everybody." There's mild applause from the audience, who are still waiting to see if Clyde Beatty is about to become the evening's entree. Carol Channing, never one to shy away from free publicity, launches into an impromptu song, while Ed attempts to go to commercial by saying, "We'll be right back with our hilarious friends from Canada, Wayne and Shuster." Ah, show business.

I would love to have been born in the era when variety shows thrived. Or maybe I should have been born a chimp. I don't think anyone has ever said to a chimp, like they've said to me, *over and over again*, "Bring it down" or "You're over the top." Has anyone ever said to a chimp, "You're hilarious, you're one of the funniest chimps on the planet. But in the right thing." Or "I need you to be more grounded, Wasu, more real."

Animal acts are timeless. Their comedy doesn't go out of fashion. This probably explains the popularity of funny cat videos on YouTube. I can watch funny cat videos for hours. Cats in paper bags, cats sleeping on the heads of dogs, cats jumping out of boxes, cats being blown by a hair dryer. Hilarious. Or how about the "Denver the Guilty Dog" video that has over 15 million hits on YouTube? Denver even has his own Facebook page.

Last night I saw a very sweet movie starring Matt Damon and Scarlett Johansson, entitled *We Bought a Zoo*. One of the zoo's employees was always seen with an adorable twelve-inch-tall monkey sitting on his shoulder. This little monkey upstaged everyone. I was star-stuck. Couldn't get enough of the little fella. At the end of the movie, when the staff are all dressed in their brown uniforms, the camera pans up to the monkey, who is wearing his own uniform, a crisp brown onesie, and no one is looking at Scarlett anymore. I can hear *aws* from the audience, but it's me who is laughing out loud. The monkey, of course, is oblivious to his wardrobe, but it's so darn dear.

I know I'm not the only person whose face lights up when she sees an animal act; animals that appear to be smiling, or can dance on two legs, or sing or talk are captivating. The great Johnny Carson used to have a returning guest on his show, an animal trainer and his talking bird. The bird's name was Howard. Johnny would engage in a conversation with the bird, but before he began he asked the bird his name, and the bird answered back in the most precise and articulate way, "My name's Howard." I don't know if it was hearing the bird talk or watching Johnny's absolute glee at hearing the bird talk that made me laugh, but I couldn't get enough of Howard the Talking Bird.

I'm going to see if I can find that on YouTube right now . . . okay, I couldn't find Howard the Talking Bird, but I found Pancho the Singing Parrot, another guest of Johnny's, and have been fixated on that video for twenty minutes. The parrot can sing "I Left My Heart in San Francisco" just as clearly as Tony Bennett and sounds like Renée Fleming warming

up. Johnny is beside himself with wonder. He is mesmer-
ized. And so am I, watching it. Great television. I miss Johnny
Carson, by the way. And Jackie Gleason and Jack Benny and
Carol Burnett. I had the honour of appearing on both *The
Tonight Show Starring Johnny Carson* in 1981 and *The Carol
Burnett Show* in 1991. Carol and I performed a *Star Trek* skit
together. You can find that on YouTube also.

I have to say, the sketch holds up after all these years, and
when I show the video in my one-woman show, it still gets

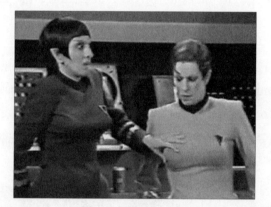

laughs. Timeless comedy. Johnny and Carol were comedic
giants and generous performers. I idolized them.

The first time I was a guest on *The Tonight Show*, I was
in my dressing room getting ready for my appearance
when there was a knock on the door. It was Mr. Carson.
He came in to tell me personally what a fan he was of
SCTV. I later found out that he never met his guests before
a show. I was deeply honoured. His respect for *SCTV* was

genuine. No one liked to laugh more than Johnny Carson. I wish I could show you the clip I have of my appearance with him. Thirty years later, you will still chuckle at his asides and inflections, and looks to Ed and to the audience. He was a master of the take, and his comedic timing was unrivalled.

When I was first booked on the show, the producer asked to show a clip from *SCTV* called "Cooking with Prickley," in which Edith stuffs a turkey with the aid of a Rhythm Ace. Mr. Carson also personally requested that he and I do a sketch together. He wanted to play Tex Boil, of Tex and Edna Boil's Organ Emporium, and he wanted me to play Edna. He had seen the characters that Dave Thomas and I created for *SCTV* and loved them. I was game, of course. How do you pass up a chance to act with the incomparable Mr. Carson? So, on national television, Johnny Carson and I performed together with no rehearsal at all.

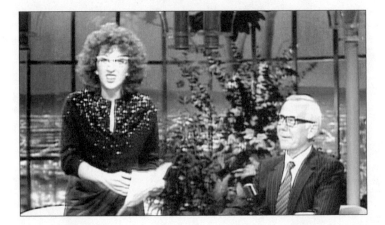

Johnny nailed it. He was loose and silly and made himself and me break up laughing during the routine. He committed to every nuance of Tex. He was utterly charming. I, on the other hand, was nervous and self-conscious, and you'd think I'd never been in front of an audience before. During the commercial breaks, he continued talking to me about his favourite *SCTV* characters and sketches. A mere three weeks later, *The Tonight Show* asked me back again. Sharing the stage with Johnny Carson that night is one of those show-biz moments I will never forget.

When I watch young comedians today, I confess, I'm in judgment mode. Not many of them make me laugh with complete abandon. Maybe it's because I'm jealous, maybe it's because I'm out of sync with their references, or maybe it's because the style in which the comedy is delivered is contrived or lazy. Maybe I'm just not smart enough to get what they are trying to say. Maybe I'm too old.

Most of the time, I watch expressionless and bored.

But give me a little dog dressed in a pink-sequined tuxedo, dancing the rumba, and I'm on the floor.

We'll be right back with our hilarious friends from Canada, Wayne and Shuster.

Months after writing this story, I filmed *Night at the Museum 3*, with Ben Stiller. I loved working with Ben because I was a long-time fan, and I couldn't wait to ask him about the monkey he had appeared with in the previous two *Museum* movies. He explained to me that the monkey was a capuchin, and her name was Chrystal. He told me that she was shy and a bit skittish, and had worked in the business for twelve years. Chrystal, he told me, was the monkey in *We Bought a Zoo.* "She is very well behaved," Ben said. "Her trainer takes great care of her; in fact, during rehearsals, she wears a diaper. When the camera is ready to roll, the trainer takes the diaper off and wipes Chrystal's bum. Chrystal stands upright and completely still in front of the crew and other actors as she prepares for her part." I thought, *That capuchin is a great actress. Chrystal knows that what she is doing is important. She is proud and uncompromising. She is the Christian Bale of capuchins. She'll do anything for her craft.* Not me. Even if the part called for it, I would not let my bum be wiped in public. There'll be plenty of time for that after I check into the Actors' Retirement Home.

My Gynecologist

Soon I'll be growing a moustache. That's what happens when a woman has too much testosterone in her body. Think Chaz Bono. My gynecologist agreed to give me testosterone after my blood tests indicated that my testosterone was low. He is giving me a prescription for AndroGel in a last-ditch attempt to increase my sex drive. Testosterone also increases your state of well-being. Horny and feeling on top of the world—what's wrong with that? Not since the 1960s have I walked around with that combination.

I exaggerate. I felt horny ten years ago when I was having an affair with Terry, my twenty-eight-year-old lover, and often times during the day, for a few minutes when my pants feel loose, I am happy. But horny *and* feeling on top of the world? Not since the first man walked on the moon.

The testosterone I'll be taking is in gel form, which is administered from a multi-dose pump. I am to dispense a small amount on my upper arm, twice a week, and in no time I'll be lifting up my blouse in front of the sexy Peruvian doorman.

I think my gynecologist is more perplexed than I am as to why I am not interested in sex, and consequently dating. Each time I see him, for my biyearly checkup, he asks me, barely audibly, "When is the last time you had sex?"

My gynecologist is a frustratingly soft talker. And I'm frustratingly hard of hearing. Usually I answer half-joking but slightly embarrassed, "I can't remember." He writes something down on my chart. I'm sure it's not *She can't remember*. That would sound very non-clinical, but it's a question he expects an answer to, and my answer always seems to disappoint him.

At my last appointment, I walked into his office and, hoping to disperse with his regular line of questioning, blurted out, "David"—I call my gynecologist by his first name, more on that later—"*I have not had any sex since the last time you asked me, so please don't ask again.*"

Not one ever to laugh at my jokes or to see the irony in them, he raised his head slightly and asked, "Why?" His pen was poised ready to write down the answer.

"Oh my God, David, I don't know. I haven't been dating, that could be the reason."

"Why haven't you been dating?" he continued seriously.

"Well, how much time do we have?"

No response from my muted, humourless gynecologist.

He means business. He's taking my love life seriously, even if I'm not willing to.

"Well," I say, taking a cue from David, and slowing letting down my guard, "maybe I'm not open to it, maybe I'm scared. Maybe I'm shy. I have always felt like Michelle Williams trapped in Joan Rivers's body. And I don't seem to have any sex drive."

"I think you're depressed," David offered.

"That could be. I *am* in between jobs." Freud said human beings need two things to make them happy: love and work. At the moment, I had neither. So maybe I was a little depressed. But that couldn't be the reason I hadn't had a sex drive for over ten years. I'd been continually employed. And in those ten years, I certainly had had episodes of prolonged happiness, albeit with an insipid libido.

Maybe Althea, my astrologer, knew the real reason I was dead inside. Venus, she told me, the goddess of love and fornication, had not appeared on my chart since my early twenties. Back then, when Venus and I were BFFs, according to Althea, I was too young to deal with Venus's erotic energy. I made bad love choices. I'm lucky, Althea says. I am going to have another chance at love before I die, because Althea tells me Venus is coming back to town—town being my chart. That's right, for most people, Venus appears once, or sometimes never, but for me, Venus appears twice on my chart. She is coming back in January, by Popular Demand. And she will stay put for the entire year.

I have to be prepared. I need a rockin' libido when I start dating again. That's why I'm willing to go the testosterone route even though, in large doses, for most women there are nasty side effects: body hair, acne, increased muscle mass, shrinking breasts. Not that bad, if I just remember to shave.

I love my gynecologist. He is brilliant and kind and attentive. I just wish he would speak louder. Now that I am older, there are many things I wish for, and they all have to do with loss. Testosterone and better hearing are just two things I wish I had more of. Taking testosterone won't cure my hearing loss, so for now, I have to read David's lips when he talks, which is challenging when his head is between my legs during my gynecological exams. This intimate act is one reason I call David by his first name. It doesn't feel right to address a man formally when he's two inches away from my vagina. The second reason we are on a first-name basis is that I'm a frequent guest at his home for Passover.

As I lie on the examination table with my legs in the stirrups and David's head lost somewhere in the abyss of my genitalia, I have to tilt my body up and stretch my head over my chest to catch a glimpse of David's mouth moving so I can make out what he is saying. And boy does his mouth move. That man knows more about a vulva than George Clooney, and he's happy to tell you everything he knows.

There is nothing more awkward, in my book, then a gynecological exam at my age. Most women, David tells me, are open to it. Forgive the pun. A couple of his patients are inhibited. One woman wears a red bandana over her eyes during the exam; other women, like me, inch their way slowly up the examination table, away from the stirrups, until their heads hit the back wall. David is understanding. Fortunately, there are cute little *New Yorker* cartoons and "Words of Wisdom" on Post-its stuck to the ceiling above us, to relax and distract us from the physical discomfort of the dreaded *Pap smear*. Just as hideous sounding as it feels.

"Ouch," I blurt out.

"Just relax," David says. "If you squeeze, it will hurt more. Stop squeezing and move your body back toward me."

I'm focused on the Post-its.

I like this quote from Plato:

Be kind
Everyone you meet is fighting a great battle.

Between the tenseness of my body and the energy it takes to decipher what David is saying, I'm exhausted after the exam. "You can get dressed now," David says as he whips off his rubber gloves, disposes of the metal torture devices, and puts my cells under a microscope to take a closer look. "Would you like to see?" At least that's what I think he asked. He might also have said, *Passover is on a Friday this year.* So I'm just guessing when I reply, "Hell, no, I am not interested in viewing my cells under a microscope. I'm an actress, not Madame Curie."

"Very good," says David. I see a smile on his face. I don't care what my cells are doing now. I got a chuckle from my gynecologist. I couldn't be more pleased.

It's bittersweet visiting my gynecologist these days. His office is filled with young pregnant women. Their life is ahead of them. And most of mine is behind me. I think of the births of my two sons many years ago when I was living in Toronto. I wasn't shy back then, lying on the examination table. I was not thinking about me. I was fixated on the health of my unborn sons and on bringing life into the world. Now I think about prolonging my life when I visit my gynecologist, and although I am enormously grateful for the care he gives me, I wish I were young again, with tons of testosterone and no discernable facial hair.

If the AndroGel doesn't work, David will come up with another solution to jumpstart my sex drive. This I am sure of. He is relentless in his dedication to his patients. And when I finally get a hearing aid, I'll know precisely what that solution is going to be.

You Are So Beautiful

And now, a forty-six-year-old perspective on *her* lady parts,* as told by Libby Wolfson, host of the daytime talk show

"You!"

Music: "You Are So Beautiful."

Libby *speaks to the camera as she lies sprawled across a mass of pillows.*

LIBBY: Hello, my name is Libby Wolfson, and today we'll be talking about menopause. There, I said it. Is it hot in here? I'm burning up, I need the Mellonville Fire Department to come hose me down. Yesterday on the set I turned up the air conditioning.

---

*Book title alert #2.

The cameraman said, "Libby, please, it's freezing."

Meanwhile, I'm feeling uncomfortable.

Next thing I know, they had to be rushed to the hospital for frostbite. I know something is wrong. So I make an appointment with my gynecologist, Wilf Steinberg. Wilf. We're on a first-name basis.

Please, after all the yeast infections, we should be buying a house together.

So, I go to his office. I say, "Wilf, I will be honest . . . My friend is irregular. Sometimes it jumps a month." I make a joke that maybe I'm pregnant. Even though it's been years since there's been any action in this vicinity. "A ghost town," I joke. "Dodge City has more visitors.

"Forget the tumbleweeds, possums could be hiding in there. First you need a can of Pledge to make a dent. Get out the DustBuster."

He's not laughing; he looks disgusted, like he could vomit from the possum analogy.

Anyway, I joke a lot. It's my way to make myself feel comfortable, because please, frankly, after all these years and many men in the '60s, I still feel violated with this kind of exam.

"Libby, please put your feet in the stirrups and relax."

Relax? The only way I could relax right now

is with a package of Milano cookies and a Stoli. Straight up.

So, I'm lying there praying he's going to tell me I have the insides of a nineteen-year-old. Suddenly, he pulls the desk lamp over for a closer look. What is he doing? Mining for gold? And I'm smelling smoke. I think my pubic hairs are on fire. With the gown draped over my knees, I could send smoke signals to the remaining Sioux.

Anyway, he finishes the exam and tells me to get dressed and we'll talk in the office. He can't tell me the bad news there.

He has to go back to his office and write in his journal, *Today I told Libby Wolfson that she has one day to live and it doesn't feel good. She's a vibrant, beautiful woman. Why didn't I ask her out when I had the chance?*

Well, fuck him. He had plenty of opportunities. So I go into his office and say, "Wilf. Wilf, please, what's the diagnosis?"

He asks me how old I am, and I tell him forty-six. He tells me I'm premenopausal.

I say, "But I don't look forty-six. Do you think I do?"

He tells me I'm not going to get my "friend" anymore. My "friend." I need the support. They don't call it "friend" for nothing. I don't want

it to go. It's the one thing I could count on
every month. I can live with the cramps. They're
life-affirming. And PMS was never really a problem. I shot my boyfriend once but got off with
the Twinkie defence.

He tells me he can put me on hormones. What am
I, Mr. Ed? Am I running the trifecta?

I can live with the mood swings. I've lived
in this body (*Crying.*) for forty-six years. I
can live with the (*Stops crying, starts laughing
uncontrollably.*) mood swings.

He tells me intercourse will be different.
He tells me this is what I have to look forward
to . . . that my vaginal lining will need something called Astroglide. What am I, a ride at
Six Flags?

Where did my thirties go? I don't even remember
enjoying them that much. What if, God forbid, I
met a man who I was attracted to and he had a good
car, and I wanted to conceive his baby? Now if I
want a child, I have to go to Malawi and buy one.

No, I want one from my own loins. I feel cheated.
I was this beautiful flower who could reproduce.
Now I produce missed opportunities. This is the
nail in the coffin. Everybody knows it.

Men don't understand. What, they lose their
hair, big deal.

I leave the waiting room, and all of these pregnant couples are sitting there, holding hands,
looking blissful. Fat but blissful. That's the
part of blissful I could do without.

Music up. Libby continues.

Is someone frying onions in here?

No, it's the unscented Mitchum mixed with the
few drops of estrogen I have left.

We'll be right back after a word from our spon-
sor, Modess Sanitary (*Libby can barely get the
words out.*) Napkins.

*We hear Libby crying as the music fades, and
the show, as well as Libby's reproductive life,
is over.*

My Astrologer

Every six months for the last eight years I have gone to Althea, my astrologer, to have my chart read. Althea is not a gypsy. She is not Romanian or Transylvanian, nor does she travel the country in a caravan. She doesn't steal babies or sacrifice cows. She's a small, round, single white woman, about fifty years old, and stands four feet, ten inches tall. And my life's decisions depend upon her every word.

Althea lives in a fourth floor walk-up. I'm always nervous to ring the buzzer when I visit Althea, in case she's in the middle of an appointment. I don't want the interruption to cause bad karma for me. Not before a reading. I usually wait until the client before me finishes his or her appointment. Hopefully, the person will exit without making eye contact with me. Making eye contact after an astrology reading is like making eye contact after a therapy session or an appointment with your dermatologist. It's always better to

leave through the back door, if there is one. You don't want
anyone to recognize you with mascara running down your
face or to see you with your newly injected lips. You don't
want to make small talk with a stranger when you can't
move your mouth.

Althea ushers me in. She is wearing a loose, faded cot-
ton housecoat. No shoes. Her toenails have not been cut for
months, and the polish on her toes has not been changed in
years. Think Gollum with a pedicure.

Every time I look at her feet, I am reminded of Howard
Hughes and his closet full of toenails that his servants stored
in jars. Althea's hair is thin and sparse, having not grown
back from her last traumatic brain surgery, her second in
a year. Her two-room apartment is dark and cramped, and
the blinds on her one window are always shut. There are no
beads or curtains hanging in her doorways. There are no
tarot cards, wind chimes, or burning sage. What there is is
a dog crate, which sits in the middle of her cluttered living
room. Books and papers are piled up the walls. Manuals,
charts, journals teeter on tables. There are flowers that have
been dead since the '70s, in vases which are nearly falling off
the mantel, which sits over a fireplace that has never been
used because bags of clothes and shoes, instead of logs, lie
piled up behind the fireplace screen.

Althea is a hoarder. Her miniature sheltie, named
Buzzy, holds a stuffed toy lobster in her mouth, and every
time someone enters the apartment, Buzzy excitedly

jumps up and down within an eight-inch radius, the only uncluttered space in which she can move. Each time I visit Althea, I notice that the walkway from her front door to the chair I will be sitting in gets narrower and narrower, and that what used to be a three-foot path is now only twelve inches wide. When I first started seeing Althea, the show *Hoarders* had not become the cult hit on cable TV that it is today. I never knew that compulsive hoarding had a name, and a diagnosis, until I started watching the show compulsively.

Since Althea lives in a spiritual world, not a material one, I believe I have no right to judge her clutter. It would be like judging Jesus's nursery. If you didn't know He was the Son of God, you might be appalled by the grazing livestock, or the frankincense stuck to the manger floor.

I wish I could be as carefree about my living quarters as Jesus or Althea. I am an obsessive cleaner. I don't know if there is a name for my obsession, but I know for sure it would not make good television. No one wants to see me fluffing pillows on my couch week after week, or positioning picture frames so they line up with each other, or polishing the marble on my kitchen countertop, or sharpening pencils so that the tips peek out uniformly from the pencils' container, or reorganizing my spice drawer alphabetically, or placing my TV and DVD remote-control wands evenly side by side in their own little remote-control box. On second thought, maybe I'll pitch my household cleaning

habits as a Web series to Proctor & Gamble, a reality program geared for women with too much time on their hands
(making a note to call them).

The truth is, I would no more have a dead flower in my
apartment for one day, let alone generations, than Althea
would have a Swiffer.

Back to astrology. Before every session, Althea asks if I
want a cup of tea. I always decline. She makes a cup for
herself and never drinks it. I guess this is just part of her
ritual. We face each other over a round wooden table. She
opens the cover of a tape recorder that she's had since the
'80s, inserts the ninety-minute cassette I have brought with
me, and turns on the machine. It runs for three seconds and
then stops. She takes out the tape, and with a pencil that
she places in one of the holes in the middle of the cassette,
winds the tape back to the beginning. All the while that she
is fiddling with the recorder, Buzzy is barking and clawing
my lap and trying to jump up, but there isn't enough space
in which to get a running start, so she just keeps turning
around and jumping anxiously in one spot. Althea is yelling, "Bad Buzzy. You're a bad girl. Do you know that? You're
a bad Buzzy. Are you going to behave?" Althea explains that
Buzzy is a Leo with a Libra moon. Buzzy wants attention.

Who doesn't? I'm thinking. *Just read what's on my chart,
Althea. The hell with the tape recorder. I'll remember all the
important stuff anyway.* Of course, I don't say this out loud,
because I don't question anything Althea says or does. She is

my mystical soothsayer and can predict my future. I'm not messing with that.

Althea hands back the tape to me. "It's not working," she says, like it's my fault. It *could* be my fault. I bought the tape at a 99-cent store. She asks me if I have an iPhone.

"Yes," I say.

"Oh good," she responds. "Let's use that."

I'm thinking, *Hmm, really? Why didn't we use the iPhone in the first place?* But again I don't question The Right Honourable Mrs. Yoda.

"Do you have a mic on the phone?" Althea asks.

"I think so."

"Is there an app for recording?"

"Oh boy, Althea, I don't know." How does this woman even know the word "app"?

"Well, let me see it."

I hand her the phone. She stares at it like she has never seen a phone before, like she would stare at a can of Comet. Buzzy is quiet because she is now on my lap. I picked up Buzzy when Althea wasn't looking, to keep her from barking and to keep Althea from yelling commands. All that exertion can't be good for Althea's delicate brain.

Althea finds the Record button on my iPhone. She presses it. She speaks into the phone as a test. It works. She gets my chart out. She lays it on her master astrology chart so that my planets line up with the universe's planets. She commands Buzzy once again to get down. Buzzy retrieves her pet lobster and quietly goes to her crate and lies down. Althea presses Record and with a reassuring smile asks, finally, after twenty minutes of my session has now elapsed, "Are you ready for some good news?"

"Yes, yes," I say. "I am really eager to hear some good news, Althea. It's only been four months since my last appointment. But I have a very specific question to ask you today. Thank you for seeing me. What do you see in my chart?"

A famous fashion designer introduced me to Althea. He had been seeing her for years. He made all his decisions, personal and career, based on her readings. He swore by her. From what I could tell, he was successful, happy, financially secure, ambitious, and thriving. How could I go wrong?

When I booked my first appointment with her, I did not know what I was going to hear, but I knew I was open to receiving what Althea saw. I wanted to put my total trust in her, because I had to. I needed positive reinforcement and direction in my life, which was fraught with anxiety and indecision. I needed to know what day to sign a contract, what agent to leave, what job to take, why I wasn't in a relationship, and how I could be a better parent. Althea answered all my questions with conviction. In fact, she has never been wrong. She is not afraid to tell me the truth, even if it is difficult to hear, but she always ends with good news. When she was learning astrology as a young girl, her teacher, renowned in the field, told her to always find something positive in a chart, and if she couldn't find anything positive, to look at Kronos, the planet of power, success, and recognition. Kronos always made a person feel good.

Well, today all eyes are on you, Kronos. Today I am here with Althea to ask if the pilot I just shot for CBS will be picked up.

Today I would like the misery of uncertainty to stop. I've been in the dark for months as CBS decides what it will order. Without this knowledge, my life is on hold. My agent and manager and industry websites—*Variety*, *Hollywood Reporter*, Deadlinehollywood.com—are just speculating. No one except the network executives behind closed doors know anything, and they're not talking . . . yet.

The stakes are high. Althea knows this. I came to her four months ago. I had been offered a Broadway musical and I was unsure about taking it because I wanted to get back to television, something I had stayed away from for the last nine years. I had been living in New York, working on the stage, on Broadway. I wanted to go to Los Angeles again for pilot season, even though I knew I was off the radar of TV casting directors, writers, and producers. I would have to reintroduce myself to Hollywood and basically start all over again. It was now or never. What was I waiting for? I had to get back on the horse. I was scared. I was stuck. So, four months ago, I booked an appointment with Althea. I asked her what I should do. I brought two ninety-minute cassette tapes, a pad of paper, and a couple of pencils and pens. I didn't want to miss a word. I wanted to get everything down: predictions from Althea, and words of encouragement and reinforcement from my buddy Kronos.

It was December. Pilot season was about to begin. Althea looked at my chart. She hesitated. "This is interesting. Do not take the Broadway play. Go to Los Angeles. I see a contract for a TV show, but it will be difficult along the way. Try not to get discouraged. There will be a lot of rejection. Do not take it personally. Do not let it affect your self-esteem. Persevere. You are going to get what you want. Work for it. Be patient. It will happen."

Well, I'm here to say, everything Althea predicted *did* happen. I went to Los Angeles. It was difficult. I had to put my ego aside and audition like I was a newcomer. There was a lot of rejection, but I persevered because I kept remembering what Althea had predicted.

Just when I was about to give up at the end of my two months in Los Angeles, I got a pilot. A good one, one I was proud of. Melissa McCarthy was the executive producer, and her husband, Ben Falcone, wrote and starred in it. Judd Hirsch and I played his parents. I loved the show, the part, the cast, the experience, and being in Los Angeles. I loved hanging out with my sons, who live there, and loved feeling visible again in an industry I had shied away from for so long.

I returned to Toronto. I waited. Nothing. Not a peep from the creators, the director, the studio, the network. I flew to New York. I called Althea. Usually it took weeks to get an appointment, but Althea heard the urgency in my voice and scheduled me in for the next day.

"Would you like a cup of tea?" Althea asked.

"No, thank you, Althea." Today I was not feeling patient or polite. *Just read my damn chart!*

"What do you think, Althea? Is my show going to get picked up for a series?" I am literally on the edge of my seat. The iPhone is on. I'm writing on a pad of paper for backup. I'm repeating everything she says.

I let her know the day that CBS is going to announce its fall lineup. May 16. "How does May 16 look in my chart?" I ask.

Althea rummages through her books and looks for my day aspects for May 16. "Ah," she says. "This is funny." Oh boy. "Funny" isn't necessarily the word I wanted to hear regarding a series pickup. She continues. "May 16 on your chart is showing me success, expansion, and recognition. It's almost impossible for the show not to go. But if for some reason it doesn't, and I think it will, but if it doesn't, it means something better out there hasn't shown up yet. I see a lot of success here. Ongoing success. You can never know for sure, but it looks good. I think it will go."

I'm elated. I don't ask her to elaborate. I don't want to tempt fate. I don't want the gods to be angry by further questioning. What she said is good enough for me. She covered it all. The series will probably go, but if it doesn't, there is something better just waiting for me. I have good reason to believe her.

This is Althea's track record with me so far:

1. She told me I was going to buy a home by the water, in Canada. I had been looking to buy a house for four years in the Hamptons, Provincetown, Maine, and Pennsylvania, but I ended up buying a beautiful little cottage on a pond in High Park in Toronto. I wasn't looking to buy a house in Canada. I just fell in love with it when I saw a For Sale sign out front, when I was visiting my sister. It wasn't until a year after the purchase that I remembered what Althea had predicted.

2. She told me I had a low-grade infection in my digestive tract. Five months later I was hospitalized for diverticulitis.

3. She told me I was going to write a book. Six months later, I had a contract with HarperCollins Canada.

4. She told me I was not going to retire. I have never had the intention of retiring. Now I have no choice.

I don't ever remember Althea being wrong. Sometimes her readings are general: You are coming on a financially lucrative few years. There is a person you know who will be offering you a job. Your self-esteem issues are holding you back. You don't really want to meet a man. You need to let your children live their own lives; stop enabling them, they will be fine. She has been correct on all counts.

Other times she has been freakishly specific. I hope she is freakishly correct this time. I would love to do a TV series. I would love to be nearer my sons.

Before I thanked Althea for her insight and encouragement, just as our session was ending, I asked her what I should do while I was waiting to hear.

"Go out and have fun. Have a good time."

I am trying to. I'm staying off the industry websites. No one knows anything. It's all buzz and hype. Only "the woman behind the curtain" knows for sure, and I'm betting on her.

Astrology Follow-Up

Well, Althea, my dear astrologer, got it wrong. At least one part of her prediction. CBS announced the series it was picking up for 2012, and my pilot was not one of them.

I was disappointed and sad. The stakes were high for this one. A lot was resting on it. I wanted very badly for this series to go. *And* I found out on Mother's Day. As I was about to go on for my Mother's Day matinee of my one-woman show in Chicago, my agent called. He, of course, didn't know I was about to go out to entertain for an hour and a half. One minute later, my sons called to wish me a happy Mother's Day. And then I hear "places" and the montage of my opening is running, and I try to pull myself together, my emotions all over the place. Disappointment that the show is not going, sadness that I am not with my sons, dismay that the theatre is not more full, and fear that I won't be able to get through my fifth performance in three days. I don't want to do my show. I'm not feeling confident, or energetic, or funny.

It's not about me, I tell myself. It's for all the people who paid, who want to laugh. All the moms who brought their children, all the children who brought their moms. My going out there today is about something bigger. Someone out there, someone you don't know, has gotten much worse news than you, Andrea. His or her plight in life is much more difficult than a series not being picked up. If you can make just that one person happy, if you can make them laugh and forget their troubles today, then do it. You owe it to them.

So I go out on stage. The house is half full. But they are by far the best audience I've had in five shows. Exuberant, appreciative, laughing at every joke. Smiles on all their faces. The show goes great. I get through it, though I am very hoarse and Seth, my pianist (and aforementioned writing coach) has had to lower all the keys. I thank the audience from the bottom of my heart. I wish them all a happy Mother's Day. I go backstage and begin to gather and pack up all my things. The stage manager asks if I will see a fan. He has been waiting patiently in the theatre. It's been forty minutes since my show ended and long after all the audience has left. I don't recognize the gentleman's name, but I say, of course I'll see him. He is escorted backstage. He stands looking at me. He is shy and hesitant. He tells me that he is a huge fan and how important it was for him to attend the show today. He tells me that his partner of thirty years, who died of AIDS ten years ago, watched *SCTV* while he was ill. It was the only thing that got him through his terrible suffering. "And you, Andrea, were his favourite. I wanted you to know what a difference you made in his life. How much joy you brought him before he died."

He hugged me. "Thank you for meeting me," he said. I held his hand.

"No, my friend, thank you for sharing your beautiful story with me. Thank you for making this Mother's Day so special for me."

The second half of Althea's prediction was this: If the series isn't picked up, there will be something better out there.

She was right. Althea, my astrologer, is always right.

Part Three

Old Lady Parts* #1

Let's get this out of the way.

I turned sixty-five recently. I know, I know, I don't look my age. At least, that's what you'll say to my face. Don't get me wrong, I love hearing it, even if I know you are blowing smoke up my sixty-five-year-old sagging ass.

I am now officially a senior citizen, which means I am entitled to a few perks, the most delicious being $4 off a regular-priced movie ticket.

In New York, you don't have to wait until you turn sixty-five to get old-age fringe benefits. Sixty-two is considered a senior citizen, so for the last three years, whenever I went to the movies in New York, I approached the box office and whispered so no one else could hear, "One senior ticket, please." Then, with the hope and naïveté of a chorus girl newly off the bus from Omaha, I waited for the response I longed for: stunned silence, followed by

*Overused title.

incredulous scrutiny, followed by *You can't be a senior, you don't look like you're a senior. You look so much younger.* Sadly, this never happened. Every time I had asked for a senior ticket, I was given one without hesitation, without a second look. Since it was so damn humiliating saying my age out loud to a self-involved, uncaring, insensitive, heartless twenty-year-old loser who one day would be sixty-five herself—and I just hope I'm alive to be there to see the devastating look on *her* mug when her age is met with no resistance—I went back to asking for an adult ticket, even though I had to pay $4 more.

But when I turned sixty-five, everything changed. It became startlingly clear how much time I had wasted in my life by indulging in fear and negativity. Now that I was sixty-five, I hopped on the yes train. *What am I waiting for?* became my mantra. Instead of comparing myself to others, I was grateful for my success, my health, all I had in my life, and I now accepted and surrendered to the number sixty-five. After all, I told myself, it was just a number.

So, four days after I turned sixty-five, I went to the movies to see *The Iron Lady,* starring Meryl Streep, at my favourite theatre in New York, the Lincoln Plaza Cinemas, where the average age of the paying customer is eighty. This time I walked up proudly to the box office and said loudly for all of Manhattan to hear, "A SENIOR TICKET, PLEASE." And then the unthinkable happened. I was asked for my ID. "I'm sixty-five, honey," I said, laughing and looking around to see if anyone else had heard the young man. "I didn't bring any proof of my age with me, but I love that you think I'm younger."

"Oh yes, absolutely, you do not look sixty-five. I can't believe it. You're sixty-five? No, really? You look (he paused as he searched for a number) fifty-four at the oldest."

"Okay, I'll take it," I said. "Julianne Moore's age! Yay, I love her," I continued. "She's so pretty with her long red hair and alabaster skin." By then I had lost him. But I continued. "My goodness," I said, now sounding like Mary Poppins, "you were brought up very well, young man, and your mother would be proud of you." Proud of him for what, making an old person feel better? Or maybe, God bless him, he thought I looked younger, and maybe I did, with my hair freshly blown out. Whatever the reason, I had not expected this attention, this lovely turn of events.

I immediately called my girlfriend. Giggling, I said, "You won't believe what just happened. The fellow who sold me my movie ticket didn't believe I was sixty-five. He asked for my ID."

"Congratulations, honey," my friend replied excitedly.

"Yeah, I'm stunned, I can't believe it. I couldn't be more thrilled," I said, sounding like I'd just been cast in a Scorsese film. Or my mammogram came back clean.

* * *

Turning sixty-five is a huge milestone, and let's be honest, even with its perks, it brings baggage: short skirts are out, dyed platinum blonde hair is out unless you live on the street or in New Jersey, being cast as the wacky girl next door is out, loud restaurants are out, loud music is out, talking about your health and sickness and death are in, old-age pension cheques are in, retirement and golf courses are in, and who cares, 'cause I hate golf, you make less money, there's less work, less sex, less fun . . . holy shit, I gotta stop. I'm depressing myself.

I hate this ageism thing. I hate feeling that everything that I have accomplished in my life is outdated, that I'm no longer viable. This is going to be my life's mission, to disprove the notion that at sixty-five it's all over.

But first, a reality check, ladies, and an honest look at the challenges of the mature woman's body.

Spanx: These are foundation garments that are supposed to give the wearer a slimmer appearance. They don't work. If you think you need Spanx, what you really need is a bigger size of outerwear. Don't waste your money on Spanx when you get to be my age. The fat has to go somewhere; it doesn't magically disappear underneath the Lycra material. The fat pops up above the waistband, or below the thigh band, giving you the appearance of the Elephant Man. *Take the Spanx off.* Your body looks unnatural in Spanx, and you still look fat.

Eyebrows: I wish I had appreciated my eyebrows more. They were bushy and Armenian and framed my big eyes perfectly. Now I have five hairs that make up my eyebrows, all growing at different angles. I don't know what happened to my eyebrows. Yes, I plucked them, but in so doing, did I destroy all the follicles? This is another body part that changes as you get older. Ears get bigger, noses get bigger, feet get bigger, and eyebrows get thinner. I guess all hair on your body gets thinner. Even my "adorkable" bangs can't conceal my straggly brows.

Hair: I regret not loving the curls on my head more. I was born with lovely naturally curly hair, kind of like Bernadette Peters's curl, soft, the silhouette almost angelic. But I wanted, like every other ethnic girl, straight Farrah Fawcett hair. And so for years I have had my hair blown out. Which at my age makes me look like Janet Reno. If I let my hair dry naturally, my curls would now look like Fran Lebowitz's, or Margaret Atwood's. Not that there's anything wrong with their curls, and they seem perfectly content with their heads of hair, but I'm more vain. And I guess more ungrateful. The older you get, the more wiry your curls, the grey roots wanting to aggressively spread to your entire head, making the texture of your hair coarser and dryer, giving you the silhouette of an angelic hedgehog.

Skin tags: Somebody has to talk about skin tags. Someone other than your dermatologist. So I will. They are ugly little things. Brown bits of skin that grow out of your neck or chest or face. On me, they pop up right above my breasts. So if a man were to rub his hand around that area, he could slice his palm in two with the brittleness of my skin tags. I have had them surgically removed. And then they grow back again. That's a lovely trade-off. Skin tags or the smell of your own flesh burning.

Gas: I think women don't talk about gas enough. No matter what I put in my mouth, it comes out my ass with the explosive sound of a nuclear warhead or a more delicate, ladylike puff of air. Just thinking of eating ice cream bloats me. And yet that doesn't stop me from eating it. It just stops me from going out after five.

Snoring: I was on vacation with my son in Sicily when he was thirteen. We shared a room at a beautifully converted monastery in Taormina. The first morning after I had woken from a very sound sleep, I noticed my son staring at me. His face was white, and he looked like he hadn't slept for days.

"Hey, honey, how long have you been up?" I asked.

"I haven't slept, Mom."

"I'm sorry," I said, concerned. "What happened? Why?"

"'Cuz you snored all night, Mom, and I couldn't sleep."

"What? I snore?" I asked, incredulous, not to mention mortified. "No one's ever told me that."

"This is how your snoring sounds, Mom: it's like a freight train coming, you hear it in the distance and then it comes around the bend full force. Every two minutes you'd rev up, stop, rev up again, and then the freight train would arrive."

"Oh, Jack, I am so sorry and so embarrassed. I don't know what to do about it. Was my mouth open?"

"Yeah, Mom, you looked like you were dead, except snoring."

"Okay, I'm getting you another room tonight."

Call me superficial, but a woman snoring is not attractive. Did Sleeping Beauty snore as she was waiting for her prince? Was she drooling as he bent down to kiss her? Every grade school child would have been traumatized for life if they saw that. Like my son has been since witnessing his freight train of a mom drooling around the bend.

Arthritis: It's really hard to disguise your age when your fingers look like Darth Vader's: spindly, swollen, and your knuckles two inches in diameter. You can't get your ring on and off unless it's sawed in two by a friendly jeweller.

Hearing: My dad lost his hearing when he was fifty. He wore hearing aids until the day he died at age ninety-two. Without them he was totally deaf. I have inherited my dad's hearing loss, even though I tell people that I lost my hearing playing in a band. That story just sounds better. But I won't get a hearing aid. It really seems like the ultimate destination in getting old. Most of the days I am angry at young people who don't articulate. The truth is, I couldn't hear them if they sounded like Dame Judi Dench.

Here's how I compensate. I read lips, but I have to be in a bright room. I can't hear (read the lips of) my dental hygienist because she wears a mask when she's cleaning my teeth. Luckily, I don't have to respond to her questions, since she has a sharp instrument in my mouth as she's asking them. I think she's used to no response. She just keeps talking in her muffled way to distract me from the pain she is inflicting on my overly sensitive gums. And while we're on the subject of gums, after my last teeth-cleaning appointment, the dentist confirmed the hygienist's suspicions. "Andrea, I think the time has come for you to consider a gum graft." Now, that term *no one* had ever mentioned to me, not one of my elderly parents, or friends, or late-night infomercials. There are ads for overactive bladders, but not yet for receding gums, thank God.

Feet: Every day I'm forced to look at my feet because it's summer and I have cute little sandals on—until you really study my feet, and then my overpriced cute little Jimmy Choo sandals don't look cute anymore. They look like receptacles for old feet.

That, and I have a hammer toe. *That's* a pretty sight. Even a toe ring in the shape of a daisy placed strategically over it can't conceal the hump. Instead, the daisy looks like it's growing out of a crag.

Eyes: It takes me an hour to get my contact lenses in. I can't figure out which is the wrong and which is the right side. And I need my glasses to see the contacts as I am putting them in my eyes. Why do they make the contact lenses so flimsy, like phyllo pastry? It's like putting a lamb-skin condom on a penis, which I would definitely need contacts for. Both have their rewards. Seeing. And seeing a hard penis.

Wisdom: I hate people who say they like getting older because they have more wisdom. Fuck wisdom. Isn't being stupid so much easier to deal with? You know what wisdom means to me? The undeniable knowledge that I'm going to die. Too much knowledge is wasted at my age.

No matter how many years I've been driving, how much knowledge I have, I'm really bad at driving now. I've actually turned into one of those women who I used to make fun of. First of all, I've shrunk. So my five-foot-three frame (which is still nothing to brag about) is now five foot one. When I drive I'm hunched over the steering wheel, all the way forward, with my head just barely seen above the wheel. When I make a signal, I move my head so much in every direction to see if there is an oncoming car that I look like a Muppet. I'm the stereotype of an older driver, anxious, impatient, slow. Yelling at cars, not good at directions, not wanting to drive at night. I cannot tell you how many times I make a wrong turn during the day. I was never good at directions, but now I'm worse even with the navigation system I have had installed. I can't program it. I need tech support just to get in the car.

Memory: I don't have one. Although my memory now is better than it was at the beginning of menopause and for that I'm grateful. Those were hideous years. Covered in sweat. Unable to remember my sister's name. Now I'm cold all the time. Fortunately, I love knitting. So that's nice. It gives me a project. Makes me feel useful and warm. Keeps my arthritic fingers moving. It enhances my eye health. The sweater I'm making covers my skin tags. Knitting is good. Knitting is this sixty-five-year-old's best friend.

Gratitude: Anyway, my body. Here's what I'm grateful for. I'm healthy, my insides seem to be working, and most of what makes me feel old no one else can see.

So, I'm gonna make the most of what I have. I'm going to use my new eyebrow pencil, which cost a reasonable $48, to draw in some lovely eyebrows. I'm going to put a hat on my wiry curls and gloves on my arthritic fingers. I'm going to put on some loose-fitting sweatpants. And I'm gonna go out for a run. Then I'm going to loudly and gleefully pass gas each time my Nikes hit the ground. The body is a terrible thing to waste.

Crazy

I am no expert on mental illness, and yet I could be, I've been called "crazy" so many times in my life. Not the Sinead O'Connor shaved-head scary kind of crazy, but the charming, spontaneous, unpredictable, cute kind of crazy. Think Diane Keaton or Goldie Hawn.

As a comedienne, I've been able to hide the varying degrees of anxiety I've suffered with all my life. Yup, I'm just a funny, wacky kind of gal. No need to run away. I won't hurt you.

I have managed my disorders successfully over the years, with exercise, therapy, family, close friends, children, a career, and humour. They are no longer debilitating. My mental-health issues now seem to be more the garden-variety, everyday neuroses that just come with living with myself twenty-four hours a day. But for millions of people who suffer with mental illness, the prognosis is more uncertain and less kind. There is still a stigma attached. We want to avoid anyone who looks and acts strange. We have little understanding and patience for people who are not like us. We are frightened to make eye contact with someone whose behaviour is different. We lack true compassion and insight. We turn away and go about our business, hoping we don't come in contact with someone who looks crazy.

Recently, I took my boots into a shoe-repair shop. They needed new rubber heels. I had never been in the store before. The tiny shop was filthy and in disarray. There were Post-its scattered all over the floor, empty bags of potato chips and candy wrappers jammed into one corner, and in another corner, I noticed what appeared to be a pile of wood shavings and sawdust. In fact, there was no section of the floor that wasn't littered with trash. There were heelless shoes piled high on a shelf in no particular order. The walls, which looked like they had been used to itemize the inventory, were marked with pencil and pen. There was no space on any counter to put my boots. The man who worked in the store was dressed fairly neatly in a black turtleneck and faded, saggy black jeans. He was in his fifties, bald, missing a few bottom teeth, and overweight. He averted his eyes as he spoke to me. His speech was halting, his manner distracted, and yet he seemed friendly enough. I couldn't hold back my shock at the state of the store, but tried.

"Wow," I said in a high-pitched voice, the customary tone I use when I'm nervous, or lying. I tried to find a place to stand.

"You don't have a lot of space in here." He made no apologies, like, *I'm sorry, I haven't had a chance to clean up* or *I've been so busy, I need to pick these things up off the floor.* He just stared at me as he stood among the worn-out bags and tired shoes and zipperless leather boots. I wanted to turn around and walk out. How could anyone in her right mind leave anything to be repaired with this man? There was no indication that he had ever repaired anything. Every item looked like it must have when it was dropped off, only now dirtier and older. The store was a disaster area. And yet I handed him my boots.

"Can I pick them up tomorrow?" I asked.

"You're the first person who has ever said they know when they want to pick up their shoes," he replied suspiciously. "I always ask and everyone says, 'I don't know, whenever.' So sure, you can have them tomorrow."

He tore a corner off a newspaper that was lying behind the counter, wrote down *#10* and *$10.00* on it, and handed it to me as a makeshift receipt. Was I the tenth customer that day, or ever?

"Umm, do you think you could clean the suede at the same time as you repair the heels?" I asked tentatively.

"No, it wouldn't work," he replied without any explanation.

"Okay, well, new rubber heels would be great, then. What time should I come back?"

"Whenever you want," he said impatiently.

He was agitated. Customers not specifying what day or

time of day they wanted to pick up their shoes was obviously a trigger for the shoe-repair guy, his Achilles heel.

"Well, how about three," I suggested randomly.

He shrugged his shoulders.

"Okay," I said, more cheerfully than was necessary, "I guess I'll see you tomorrow at three."

He was no longer looking at me. His attention was on a rubber band he was trying to put around my boots—*The boots I might never see again,* I thought. Tomorrow I'll come by and the store will be shut down by the city as a health hazard. Or maybe it's really not his store. It's a deserted shop and he just dropped by, broke in, and was pretending he owned the place. Wow, I've seen way too many movies. *The Fisher King* comes to mind.

Why did I leave the man my boots and not take them to another shoe-repair shop? Because I was overcompensating for my discomfort at being in the presence of someone who was, and yes, I'm projecting, mentally ill. Not that he wasn't functioning, showing up for work, and able to make a living. Of course, I know nothing about this man other than the brutally quick judgment I made based solely on his appearance. Just because this man's store was filthy and he couldn't look me in the eye didn't mean he was insane and was going to beat me to death with a sandal. Maybe he was just quirky and was happy in clutter. For all my talk about tolerance toward the mentally ill, I am just as uncomfortable as the next guy when I'm in contact with someone who doesn't appear to be "normal." I didn't want to show any discrimination toward this man, so I left my boots with him. I was going to prove to myself that I am a compassionate soul who would go out of her way to help someone troubled and less fortunate. The point is, I'm a hypocrite.

I loved the therapist character Patricia Clarkson played in the movie *Lars and the Real Girl*. The therapist believed that unconditional love and acceptance could heal even the most tormented and fragile soul like Lars. And in the movie, they do. She and the whole town rally around Lars and accept his delusional behaviour, until finally he feels safe enough to be able to let it go. Of course, I want to believe, as David O. Russell's film *Silver Linings Playbook* illustrates, that there is someone for everyone, and when that person finds the right person, love conquers all, even mental illness. Look, I'm not naive. I know that falling in love isn't going to cure schizophrenia, nor can it stop a deranged person with a gun. But television and film are now making it "acceptable" to talk about mental health. They are removing the stigma. I admired Robert De Niro's courage as he broke down and cried on Katie Couric's show when he acknowledged his son was bipolar. Howie Mandel was a guest on CNN recently and shared openly his lifelong struggle with OCD. Just like Michael Moore did in his film *Sicko*, where he exposed the injustices in the US health care system, filmmakers are helping us look at mental illness in a kinder, educated, more compassionate way.

The next afternoon, punctually at three, I picked up my boots. They looked really good. As I was handing the gentleman my $10 I asked him if he was the shop owner. "Yes," he said, "since 1978."

As I was leaving, I noticed a sign in the window: John's Shoe Repair Shop—The Longest-Running Shoe Repair Business in the City.

Some Things I Think About but Don't Say Out Loud

I don't trust fat therapists.

I pretend to like all wild creatures.

I could watch gorillas pick bugs off their heads for hours.

I can't stop looking at JLo's ass.

I obsessively buy books and don't read them.

My headshots are airbrushed so much, even *I* think I've had work.

I can't wait to get my bathrobe on.

I can't read a script without falling asleep.

I talk to myself out loud. It's reassuring and keeps me company.

I judge people by the colour of their teeth.

I've seen Tom Stoppard's play *Arcadia* three times and still don't know what the hell he's talking about.

Wait, why is King Lear upset? 'Cause he's old and can't trust his daughters?

I would like to have sex with every boy who works at the Genius Bar.

Dogs wearing shoes make me happy.

I used to tie my poodle's ears together. He liked it, really.

In the '80s, I danced nude in my living room but it took a Quaalude to do it.

I love going to a really depressing foreign film at three o'clock in the afternoon. It feels good to cry with ten strangers over age sixty.

Tina Fey mentioned me in her book, and it boosted my self-esteem. For a minute.

Why So Angry, Ms. Martin?

Here's what a contemptuous flight attendant with a patronizing attitude just announced over the intercom: "Look outside your windows now. What do you see? Clouds. That's exactly what you'll be seeing for the next four hours. So lower your shades so that everyone can see the TV screen."

First of all, Ann Coulter, I like looking at clouds. And second, I paid as much as everyone else on this flight and I'm keeping my window shade open, thank you very much.

And another thing, why can't I use the first-class washroom if I'm flying coach? I have a first-class vagina and I pee like everyone else. Do I really have to pay more to empty my bladder?

I take a deep breath. This trip is leading me to serenity.

Twice a year, I take a flight cross-country to Escondido, California, where I spend seven glorious days at the Golden

Door. Some might call it a spa. I call it a spiritual rehab, a physical reboot camp. However you slice it, by the time six months roll around again, I maniacally count the days till I can get back to my precious Golden Door.

I'm on a JetBlue flight from JFK right now. It's been over nine months since I visited the Golden Door this time around, and I am in bad need of a fix. This is my first opportunity for a vacation since opening in *Pippin* on Broadway seven months ago. After performing eight shows a week on a trapeze, I'm worn out. My nerves are shot. My body aches. My back is in spasm. My feet have corns from dancing in boots. My hair has no lustre from wearing wigs. My skin is wrinkled and dry from applying makeup nightly. I look like an apple doll.

I can't wait for the next seven days: hiking, meditation, sun, yoga, fresh vegetables from the Golden Door's organic garden. I'm kinda even looking forward to the choco-late mousse cake, which is, incredibly, prepared with avo-cado. No cream or flour in that baby. Healthy and yummy. Everything tastes good at the Golden Door because some-one other than me has made it. And this week is a special focus week, a bonus. It's Inner Wisdom Week, and besides the exercise, massages, and facials, I will have the oppor-tunity to sit with ten other women in a daily Wise Woman Circle and learn invaluable happiness skills as I look within. Who thought it took skill to be happy?

* * *

Two loud, whining, hyperactive kids sit in the seats next to mine. Their mother sits in the same row, on the other side of the aisle. She is playing Fruit Ninja on her iPhone and is ignoring her kids. They are hitting each other. The younger kid cries as the older one pushes him off his seat. They want attention. *Give me that iPhone,* I want to say to the mother, *I'll show you how to slice a watermelon. Get back to your children. They need you.*

Funny, having raised two kids of my own, how little to no patience I have for other children. I want to stuff my almond croissant, the one I purchased for $5 back in the terminal, down their squealing throats to shut them up. I remember the many trips I took with my kids when they were little. I guarded them as if I were an FBI agent.

My kids never spoke above a whisper. They never kicked the seat in front of them, or repeatedly unlocked the food tray, or constantly hit the seatbelt buckle against another person's armrest, or played ball in the aisle, or poked a loud video screen of mindless games for hours on end. I kept them entertained for the duration of each and every flight. I brought Cheerios in little resealable bags that kept them occupied one Cheerio, one happy moment, at a time. I brought stacks of colouring books and crayons. I read to them. I helped them build little men and the little men's horses out of Lego. I sang to them, held them, rocked them, escorted them to the bathroom, and cleaned up after every spill. They were quiet and well-mannered and felt excited, not entitled, to travel. Yes, I was drained after a day of flying, but it felt good knowing my kids and I helped to ensure that the other paying passengers had a stress-free flight. And I came off heroic. Who doesn't like that? The passengers were grateful. And that was worth it to me even though I looked like the living dead as I crawled off the plane.

The kid next to me is now complaining to his mother about his seat. He doesn't like being in the middle. Who does, kid? You're five. You don't have a choice. He is yelling that he wants my window seat, the one I booked months ago so that I would have control over the window shade when the flight attendant asks, ten minutes into the trip, if I can lower it so the other passengers can better see their television screens. Unlike the other passengers, I will not be watching my television. I will be reading my book, god damnit, the Dalai Lama's *The Heart of Compassion*. I hope to achieve this state in the next seven days at my spiritual retreat. And to get a head start on compassion, I'll need the fucking window shade open to do it.

The mother is not paying attention to her demanding son. She has now put her phone down to ask the flight attendant if her daughter, who is sitting in the last row of the plane with her husband, can sit up front with her.

"There's nothing we can do, ma'am," says the flight attendant. "The plane is full, and all seats have been assigned."

The mother turns to me now and asks me if I would mind giving up my seat so her daughter can sit up front with her.

First of all, *NO, over my dead body*, I uncharitably think of her unreasonable request. No one's switching, okay, Ms. Needy? So stop pleading.

Second of all, I paid an additional $60 for my "even more space" seat. That means I have two additional inches of precious real estate that I ain't giving up. Besides, her daughter is in the middle seat in the last row of the plane. Does this woman think I'm crazy? Does she think I'm Mother Teresa? Who would give up a bulkhead seat with extra legroom to sit in the middle of the last row, the pee-and-poo row closest to the toilet? Maybe the Dalai Lama. And maybe after I finish his first chapter on kindness I will revisit the seat-swapping quandary. But for now, *Selfish* is my mantra.

"No," I say to the manipulating mother, "I'm sorry, but I'm claustrophobic and need to be by an open window at the front of the plane."

The woman looks at me in disbelief and with disdain. I could strangle her and rip her phone out of her hands so she will never ever be able to split a kiwi apart again. The war is on.

The flight attendant is making an announcement now that someone on the flight has a peanut allergy. I remember I have packed a bag of homemade trail mix with me so that I won't be tempted to eat the prepackaged processed sugary snacks the airline provides. I have yummy walnuts, raw cashews, organic almonds, and ginger pieces in my little bag. I came prepared. The mother indignantly blurts out that her son, the seatbelt- and food-tray assaulter, is also allergic to peanuts.

Averting my eyes from the mother, I inform the flight attendant that I have other nuts in my purse but not peanuts.

"That's okay," she says, "it's the dust from the peanuts that people are allergic to."

"Wait a minute," says the enemy, with whom I am gearing up for full-blown combat, "my son is *also* allergic to walnuts."

"Oh," says the flight attendant, looking apologetically at me, "but it's just when he ingests them, right?"

"Listen," says the mother, "I don't want to have a fight over this. I said he's allergic to walnuts."

I am now holding back a viper's store of venom. My voice is pinched. My mouth is brittle. I am perched in seat 8F, ready to kill.

"Well, then I won't eat my walnuts," I say belligerently. "I won't eat any of the nuts I brought with me. I'll keep them sealed in a bag, away from you. Don't you worry. No one will see or taste or feel my nuts for the next five hours."

I am appalled at my lack of courage. I surrendered so easily. I'm weak. I can't even stand up for a few unsalted cashews.

The mother goes to the back of the plane to check on her husband and daughter. The kid closest to me is now jumping up and down on his seat and hitting my headrest.

He kicks his knapsack on the floor and it lands on my shoe-less feet. I have a ritual when I fly. I take off my shoes. Put them neatly in my carry-on. Put on some cozy socks. Place a tennis ball behind my back, and I'm ready to fly in comfort. I whip around to face the kid. My eyes are fixed on his as I mouth the words, in slow motion, clearly and menacingly.

"Sit. Down. Now."

He looks back at me stunned, but he obeys and sits. I keep staring at him. He is frozen. My eyes could burn a hole in his Spider-Man hat. I wish I'd brought my Valium with me, the two left from last year's surgery. I'd have no trouble dropping them into his juice box.

Okay, now I'm verging on child abuse.

I could be arrested for this, though the brilliant comedian Paul Lynde was not apprehended on a Southwest flight when he said to the mother of a screaming child, "You shut that kid up, or I'll fuck it."

Who am I? Has my darker self, the evil Mrs. Hyde, taken over? The caring Dr. Jekyll in me loves kids. I, the one-time Canadian ambassador to UNICEF; I, the woman who fostered a Haitian child for ten years; I, the spokesperson for COAF, the Children of Armenia Fund; I, a kids' mentor at performing arts organizations all around North America; I, a camp counsellor at the Luther Gulick camp in Maine for five summers in a row. I, the mom of two kids she loves madly and unconditionally and would put herself in front of a train to protect.

Have I turned into that kind of cranky old woman who overnight becomes irritable, irrational, short-tempered, and abrupt? Am I now the woman I thought I'd never be? The crotchety spinster sitting on her front steps in a rocking chair, yelling at the neighbourhood kids to get off the lawn?

Airline travel could drive anyone insane. I know it's a dull and boring conversation—how flying isn't what it used to be—but I'm going to risk being boring and reminisce. Let me take you back to a time when flight attendants were called stewardesses, passengers smoked in their seats, and sharp knives were not considered weapons. If you were fortunate enough to travel in first class, as the cast of *SCTV* were, you were given bottles of wine or champagne during the flight, roast beef was carved on linen-clothed tables in the aisles, and you ate with real silverware.

I loved travelling with the cast, and no one was more fun to travel with than John Candy. Even though we were all treated equally on the plane, he demanded the most respect and was given it. Everyone loved John and felt elevated in his presence. No one was more generous than John to anyone, anywhere. Or more grateful. He was boisterous and lively and indulgent. Booze flowed, food was abundant. John made everything into an event. Nothing and no one seemed to bother John. He loved people. He didn't feel threatened. He was an open vessel, a free spirit, an innocent kid. I wonder what he would be like if he were sitting next to these children and their mom. First of all, he wouldn't be judgmental.

He would engage in play with them, make them laugh. The mom would adore him. The father would have traded seats with some kind soul so he too could be in John's presence. John would probably find the kids delightful, not annoying. And then he'd hold court. A crowd would gather. He'd be in the moment, not even thinking of what the next five hours would bring. John would make the flight into his own personal party, and everyone on the plane would be invited. He was a volcano of joy. It's no wonder the whole world still misses him. John ate, drank, and danced happiness. He didn't need a week at the Golden Door to develop *that* skill.

If I can just keep a lid on my judgmental, fearful, ego-driven Mrs. Hyde for the next three hours, I'll be in the loving arms of the Golden Door, where my enlightened and compassionate Dr. Jekyll will feel safe to emerge. I know that, at my core, I'm kind. It's my neurotic personality that gets in the way. For now, I'll practise deep breathing. I'll take my bag of nuts to the washroom, a nut-safe zone, and I'll savour each and every one of them. For the next seven days, after all, I am going to be meditating and hiking and doing yoga and journaling and having hot stones placed on my aching back. I will have finished Mr. Lama's book on compassion. I will have perfected the art of happiness. Nothing will bother me again.

* * *

I arrive at the Golden Door.

It's beautiful. First thing up: yoga. Then, counting the minutes to lunch. I'm so hungry. And boy do I need a cup of coffee. And while we're at it, a TV. So limber and yet so hostile. No chocolate within miles. I'm famished. I'm about to boil my belt. Get me out of this Zen hellhole. I'm not meant for this relaxation thing. Deepak Chopra, my ass.

Monday, Tuesday, Wednesday, finally I start to unwind . . . seven days later. Surrender, serenity, gratitude, bliss.

Armed with my newfound happiness skills, I board the plane. Kinder, and more compassionate, to myself and to others.

With an open heart, I lower my window shade.

Ten minutes later, I open it again.

Rome wasn't built in a day.

The Graphologist

I had my handwriting analyzed by a graphologist recently at a birthday party.

She asked us to write out our names, and then she interpreted our signatures. The birthday girl instructed the graphologist, Paula, not to alarm anyone with what she saw. The way in which someone wrote a *g*, for example, might indicate that person was a serial killer, and no one wanted to spend the evening in fear of being strangled in the powder room. Paula could also tell by your handwriting if you were confused about your sexuality and/or you were a liar and a thief. In fact, companies hired her all the time to screen prospective employees. She looked for traits of honesty, reliability, and intelligence, and the ability to be happily exploited. For instance, would you be content with a small desk and an office with a partition but no real wall? Her track record, she proudly stated, was great. She travelled the world and was hired by corporations, government, and spas—and for birthday parties.

She showed us Donald Trump's signature, which was thick and persistent. It was written with a heavy hand and heavy ink. It looked like a locomotive in motion. Jacqueline Kennedy's signature was neat and pretty, but Paula said it showed aloofness. I liked it because it was legible. Osama bin Laden's signature was ornate and insistent and confident and scary. It looked like the writing of a madman. Albert Einstein's was small and didn't take up too much space, yet he changed the world. We were all impressed and excited to see what our names would reveal.

She kept her analysis very short and complimentary.

"Very, very smart," Paula said as she studied the way I wrote my name.

"Creative, independent, very literary. You are a writer." That was *really* reassuring, having just signed a book deal. She was about to move on but stopped abruptly and blurted out a zinger. "Oh dear. Look at the way you cross your *t*. You are very, very sensitive to what people say about you professionally, and personally you have a tendency to be defensive." And then she cheerfully went on her way to analyze the nervous woman on my right.

"Wait just a moment," I said defensively. "I don't think I'm that way at all. I've worked hard not to care about what people think of me. Is there something I should be doing differently when I write my name? Should I change my signature?"

Paula, who had twelve more women to get to, ignored my line of questioning, smiled knowingly, and creepily moved on. *Maybe* she's *a serial killer,* I thought. No one would ever know. Who could read handwriting in *that* group, a bunch of drunk women over fifty? Besides, what Paula said was bullshit. She was, after all, an elaborate party favour, one step above a singing telegram.

In any case, I took down her number. I also chose not to walk back to my car alone.

Wherever You Go, There You Are

'm already planning my escape. I am huddled in the guest bedroom, checking my watch every ten minutes. I have been up all night, not able to sleep in my new surroundings. I am the guest of a husband and wife, two doctors I met in New York. They are lovely, generous, intelligent people, and it's always fun to dine with them in Manhattan, which is really the only socializing we have ever done.

They invited me to stay at their beautiful sprawling farm in Maine. Even though I grew up in Maine, I have never spent time in farm country, and I thought this would be a wonderful opportunity to see more of the state and have a little excursion at the same time. They own a working organic farm along the northern coast. Guinea hens roam freely around their 135 acres, goats munch on grass to keep the ticks away. Belted cattle graze in the distance. Vegetables and herbs sprout everywhere. It is late May, and the lilacs are still in bloom this far north. There is a wooden wraparound porch, a stone labyrinth by the front door, unspoiled vistas, and miles and miles of manicured lawns as far as the eye can see. It is green, bountiful, expansive, peaceful, idyllic. But my only thought is *When the hell can I get out of here?*

I arrived just yesterday evening, at five o'clock. I pulled my car into the gravel driveway and instantly panicked. I wanted to back up and speed away before my hosts could see me. In hindsight, I should have made some excuse when I landed in Portland, something like, *My plane was delayed and now I really think it's too late to drive the two hours, by myself, to your farm.* But instead, I got in the car and drove the two hours. At the time, I was proud of myself for honouring the invitation and not copping out. But that was last night. Now it's 6 a.m. and I'm exhausted. I haven't slept. I need a cup of coffee. Do I stay in my room until the proper hour? What *is* the proper hour to leave my bedroom and go down and get a cup of coffee? I've got the chamber of commerce free magazine *Discover the Jewel of the Maine Coast* next to me on the bed, and I'm mapping out my next destination, if I can just sneak out and, like El Chapo, hide myself in the laundry basket, get in my car, and speed away. Then I could find a cute little café, sip my latte, and sit alone blissfully.

I'm not a prisoner here. I could leave of my own accord. Steve McQueen is not my cellmate, though I wish he were still alive and we were sharing this room. It's not like I have to dig my way out of a tunnel using a metal utensil. I am a free agent who could easily go downstairs and make a cup of coffee and wait for her hosts to get up. Or maybe they *are* up. I'm too scared to find out. And yet I really need caffeine. Maybe they are still sleeping and I won't have to make conversation. I am the house guest from hell.

I think it's a morning issue. I need to get my bearings before I start the day. I need solitude, to arrange my thoughts. What do I think is going to happen if I just tell them how I feel, that I'm tired and in need of privacy? I think every host should be required to put a *How to Be a Good Guest* manual in each room. Then we would know what was expected of us. Airlines give you guidelines. *Put your seat backs in the upright position. Fasten your seatbelts. Shut off all electronic gadgets. I'm speaking to you, Ms. Martin, in seat 3F, you with the iPhone 5, whose light you are trying to conceal by putting the phone under your leg so you can type one last text before the flight attendant walks by.*

It would be so comforting to have direction. Everyone would be on the same page.

I wish the following guidelines had been left on my pillow last night:

Dear House Guest,
1. Come downstairs anytime. You will not be disturbing anyone.
2. Pour yourself a cup of coffee.

3. No one will speak to you unless you speak first.
4. Go back to your room.
5. Shut the door.
6. Please return your used coffee cup and put your tray
   in the upright position.

Have I lived alone too long? Am I just no longer flexible? No adventure left in my gypsy soul?

I didn't used to be like this. I've travelled and lived in many places.

Paris, for two years. Morocco for six months. Missouri for one year. Boston for two. Maine, Toronto, Los Angeles, eighteen years in each place over the span of sixty-five years. Been there, done that.

But now I'm planning my escape. Who am I? Django Unchained? To escape what? Me?

You know what they say: "Wherever you go, there you are."

Fuck them. Who are *they* anyway? Some bohemian acid-tripping writer from the '60s? Who coined that phrase?

The Maine Eastern Railroad has an excursion in the summer. Sounds like so much fun. And I can do it alone. Be on the train for two hours as it travels from Rockland to Brunswick. In a restored antique car. And seniors travel for only $17 round trip. I am now one of the seniors I see pictured in all the train brochures, but with darker roots, and outrageously expensive highlights. This is my next fun adventure. A really slow two-hour train trip in which the train travels one mile every fifteen minutes. Chipmunks walk faster. But at least I'll be able to spot one.

At 6 a.m. the next morning, I escaped. Yay for me. I'm in a bed and breakfast in Boothbay Harbor, Maine. Alone. I left the farm early. My hosts were very understanding as I lied and said I was called back to New York for a meeting. I had a good night's sleep. I feel rested and restored and inspired to write and explore. I have a crisp white flannel bathrobe on, compliments of the inn, left for me in my cozy little room. I just poured myself a cup of coffee from my very own coffee machine. Birds are gently tweeting outside the sliding French doors, which open to a tiny balcony overlooking the harbour. It is gorgeous. Quiet before the tourists awake and begin walking up and down Main Street. My favourite time of the day. I feel bad about lying. What a cowardly thing to do. Maybe I'll write my host and hostess a letter, in which I'll tell them the truth.

> *Dear Host and Hostess,*
>
> *I had only two days in Maine, and once I arrived, I realized that I'd like to take some time by myself, exploring the towns along the coast. I'm writing a book, and I think travelling to old familiar places might jog my memory and help fill in the blank spaces of my past.*

Thank you for sharing your beautiful home with me. You are exceptional hosts, and I am so grateful you asked me here. Until our next dinner in Manhattan, where as soon as we're finished eating I can return to the comfort of my own apartment, I remain, in gratitude,

Andrea

I will never send it.

And now it's time for my delicious free continental breakfast. I walk into the dining room and am greeted by the sombre, mannish innkeeper.

First I ask her politely if I can have a late checkout, just thirty minutes more so I can leave at 11:30 instead of at 11:00.

With a feigned smile she replies, "No. We have to do the sheets."

I continue cheerfully, "Would there be any way *my* sheets could be collected thirty minutes later?"

Still smiling insincerely, she replies, "No."

I then ask if she knows of a hair salon that's open that morning.

"There's Capella's, a ten-minute drive, but they might be closed."

"Oh," I say pleasantly, "do you think you could call and find out for me, especially since you know the people?"

"No," she says, "I'm leaving right after breakfast. But *you* could phone later."

The final exchange goes like this:

Mannish innkeeper: We are serving a mushroom quiche and a blueberry cobbler this morning. Please let me know if you have any allergies.

Me: The quiche sounds wonderful. But are there onions in it?

Mannish innkeeper: Yes.

Me: Oh, I can't eat onions. Would you be able to make one without onions for me?

Mannish innkeeper: By allergies, I mean gluten-free, or lactose intolerant, or diabetic, but not something you don't like. There's a difference between allergies and food you don't like.

Me, *through clenched teeth:* Oh, I see, well, thank you for your help, mannish innkeeper. I'll have the quiche, pick out the onions, eat rapidly, return to my room, pack between phone calls to hair salons, shower, and check out, so that I can be back on the road in thirty minutes.

Wherever you go, there you are.

Part Four

Parapharyngeal Abscess

For whatever reason, and I'm sure only the Lord above knows why, out of the blue I got a terrible strep infection that abscessed deep inside my parotid gland and then deeper inside my jaw, behind my ear. On June 15, 2012, three days before I was scheduled to perform my one-woman show *Final Days, Everything Must Go!* in the new cabaret space at the legendary club Studio 54, I was rushed to the hospital with a high fever and excruciating pain. I stayed in the hospital for five days as tests were run. The doctors finally determined that I had a parapharyngeal abscess in my neck and needed an operation. In my hospital bed as I awaited surgery, and dreamily sedated with Valium and Percocet, God's candy, I wrote the following email:

My darling male friends, and Deb,
I am going to attempt to bring you all up to date.

It is 7:40 a.m., day five at the hospital. I'm in my cubicle. Anne Frank's room was bigger. But at least I don't have to share it with an entire Jewish family.

I am supposed to have surgery today, or as they euphemistically call it, a procedure. The most handsome Israeli doctor, the head, no pun intended, of the Head and Neck Surgery Department at the hospital, just left my room. If I weren't so hard of hearing, I would have been soothed by his soft-spoken manner. Immediately I felt confident when he started to speak. First of all, he sat on a chair in front of me and looked into my eyes, which none of the attendant physicians had done. They always enter en masse, like they're in a Seth Rogen film, and stand around my bed, then one person speaks and the rest just stare. But this doctor sat like we were having cocktails, and though he had twenty-eight surgeries scheduled for the day, I felt like I was his only patient. I love an Israeli man. Sexy. Swarthy and good in combat. He explained that the kind of infection I have and where it is in my mouth is rare and very serious. He asked me if I had been in a foreign country in the last year where I might have contracted TB. I said no, and then thought maybe the Playbill cruise Broadway on the High Seas was the culprit. Maybe as I was performing Prickley in Corfu, a Greek bug flew in my mouth. Whatever the cause, the result is crazy pain that has gone on now for twelve days. The infection is deep inside my mouth/head, and so they have to give me general anesthetic, not a local, which would be so much easier to recover from.

I am on a waitlist for surgery. Or in show-biz terms, a shortlist. Think of it this way: they have asked for my availability. So I don't know when the surgery will be scheduled, but I do know I can't eat or drink anything until they do it. I can't have coffee, and so my head is pounding from the lack of caffeine. They brought me a sponge on a stick and dipped it in water, and I use that to swab my mouth. That's what's on the menu for today.

When they do the surgery, they will make an incision in my neck. They will then work their way to the infection, drain the abscess, put in a plastic tube, leave it there for two days, and do a biopsy on the tissue, sending it to a laboratory to find out if a tumour is the cause of the infection. I will then stay in the hospital for three or four more days as I heal, and then they will close the incision. That's if everything goes well.

I know this is more information than any of you, my actor friends, should know, even an actor who has played a doctor on television. But I wanted to give you sweet people in my life the whole picture. Of course, this is only part of the picture.

I had an MRI yesterday. They put a blindfold over my eyes, stuck my head in a tight-fitting helmet, then moved my entire body into a machine that looked like a tunnel, and for forty-five minutes, and I'm not exaggerating, my head became a construction site of loud incessant jackhammers and drills pounding in my ears. Honestly, if it hadn't been for the years of meditation technique I learned at the

Golden Door, I don't think I would have survived it. I kept breathing calmly, counting, thinking of my sons and, occasionally, why the hell I couldn't get an audition for the role of Miss Hannigan in *Annie*. Waterboarding would have more pleasurable.

When I finally was taken off the table, I said to the technician that the procedure was torture, and he replied, "I'll tell you what torture is: having dinner with my son."

There's a lovely elderly toothless lady named Miss Cooper, who brings me my food. I don't want to be mean because I know the entire nation of Africa would call this five-star dining, but honestly, it is swill. Maybe that's a good thing, since I can't chew, so why be tempted? I was thinking also that it's a blessing that I'm not dating because I would not be able to service any fella's penis right now. The only thing my mouth can open wide enough to blow is a toothpick.

As many of you know, who might have purchased tickets for my New York debut at 54 Below, I had to cancel. I am still laughing, not an open-jawed laugh but an internal one, at Scott Wittman's remark. When I was crying and telling him how bad and embarrassed I felt about cancelling, he said, "Oh, for God's sake, it's cabaret, one step above a flea circus." I love you, Scotty, for that. And Nicky, our darling friend in a wheelchair, offered to help. He called and said whatever I needed; he could be there in a little over two hours.

My dear BFF, my angel, Deb Monk, has been by my side from the moment I entered the hospital. Last night when I got the results of the MRI, I was distraught and scared and crying. Deb, in the most compassionate manner, held my hand and whispered, "I'm cancelling everything tomorrow to be with you." Snapping out of my distress, I said competitively, "What the hell do you have planned for tomorrow?" She then showed me her calendar, and sure enough, she is going to cancel her walk.

And Sean Hayes, my darling, thank you for your heartwarming email:

> *I'm* abscessed *with your infection. Abscessed. I can't stop researching it.*

> *I so want to be there when they cut that fucker open and watch all that shit come out of you. There'd be nothing more satisfying. It's like you have a constipated boil in your jaw. Love it. All right, joke's over. Get better already. We love you.*

Seth and James have texted me every second, and I adore the updates on their busy lives and hate that I'm not decorating their apartment and picking single socks off the floor. The thought of buying chairs and carpet and wiping out their saving accounts is keeping me going.

Nathan, thank you, my sweet angel, for the call, the cookies, and the personal appearance in my hospital quarters. All the nurses recognized you, and because of that I got more melted ice cream at lunch.

Okay, now this is sounding like some acceptance speech.

Fuck all of that.

Just know, Sean, Scotty, Nicky, Victor, Scott, Marc, Nathan, Seth, and Deb, I love you. Thank you for being the best crew I have ever worked with.

Wait.

Thank you for being my friends.

Later that day, after sending out the email, I received a slew of responses from my friends. I won't reprint all of them, but Marc Shaiman's in particular was priceless:

You may have got a terrible infection, but you also got your new act. Where the hell were you when *Catch Me If You Can* needed a punch-up?

Well, I hope to God you are at least going to make use of the time under and have them do a little cleanup work. Hopefully not by the Israeli doctor, for he might read the instructions you write out for him backwards and end up *lowering* your face and tits.

* * *

My surgery, which took four hours, was scheduled for the following day. As I was about to be wheeled into the operating room, my oldest son, Jack, appeared. He had flown on the red-eye from Los Angeles to be with me.

"Hi Mom, it's Jack," he whispered. "Everything's gonna be all right. I'm here now. I love you." He held my hand. "I'll see you when you get out."

The pain in my jaw was so intense by then, I couldn't speak. I wanted to yell, "Hey, nurses, doctors, patients, this is my son Jack. He is a music editor and just finished a big movie and isn't he handsome?" Instead, I squeezed his hand as tears ran down my swollen cheeks. Jack's smiling face was the first I saw when I got out of surgery. Jack stayed with me in New York for two weeks after I left the hospital, and made me laugh continually by pointing out that I looked like Mrs. Cartman on *South Park* because one side of my face was paralyzed and only the right side of my lip curled up.

After a six-week recovery period, I could move every part of my face again. Seven weeks later, I was starring in a Hallmark Movie of the Week, and eight weeks after that, I was training on a trapeze. I'm happy to report that the surgery was a success. I'm completely healed. The four-inch incision on my neck has faded and now looks like an eyebrow in a Hirschfeld drawing. When I smile, I no longer look like a character in an animated cartoon. My life-threatening infection is a thing of the past. I don't talk about it anymore. Not because I'm not grateful to my doctors and friends and family for their concern, expertise, love, and devotion. And not because it doesn't make a dramatically harrowing story.

I just can't pronounce "parapharyngeal."

Emergency

"Damn," said the emergency room nurse. "Your vein exploded."

She gathered up her needles, tape, and vials and stormed out of my curtained-off cubicle in the emergency room at the hospital where I had just been admitted. I followed her out to the nursing station, where she was asking a male nurse if *he* knew how to draw blood.

"Umm, excuse me," I said, "that sounds bad." *An exploded vein. What will happen to me now? Will the rest of me explode?*

Angrily she responded, "It will hurt for a few days, and you'll have a black-and-blue mark and bruising on most of your arm."

I waited for even a suggestion of an apology. None came. She commanded me back into the cubicle, and to sit and not move as she pulled out another set of pain-inflicting tools. She took hold of my arm, with its now ballooning vein. I tried another mode of communication, the "I hope you recognize me and will treat me more kindly 'cause I'm an actress and I'm shooting a TV series, so it would be great if you would be gentle and maybe use a needle that you use for children, 'cause I don't want to have bruises on *camera.*" No acknowledgement. Nothing.

"That's what I *am* using," she snapped back. "Now sit and stop clenching your fist." She stuck the needle in the front of my hand this time and wistfully smiled.

"Damn," she said, "you have beautiful veins." Even that was my fault. I had disappointed her. I had allowed my beautiful veins to be exploded. She finished drawing blood and left the cubicle. I then overheard her joking loudly with three other nurses in the hallway. "So anyway, he touched me and then he stuck his tongue down my throat." Gales of boisterous laughter in the hallowed halls of emergency. "I didn't even know him. But hell, he was cute, and I was hammered, so I stuck my tongue right back down his."

By now both injection sites on my arm were turning purple. Soon I would look like the Elephant Man. "I'm a human being, Nurse Ratched," I wanted to yell, "not an animal." But instead I asked tentatively through the curtain, "When will the doctor be by?"

She yelled back, "I don't know. He's busy."

I had driven myself to the emergency room at 7 a.m. that morning. At 2 a.m. I had woken with sharp pains and a tightening in my chest. I paced around my home for five hours, all the while moaning and scared. When I finally went back to bed, I was convinced I smelled toast and was having a heart attack, so I drove myself to the hospital. And there I sat for the next five hours. X-rays of my heart, EKGs, blood samples, and a CT scan of my lungs showed nothing irregular. And yet I couldn't breathe. And the pain was not subsiding. As I waited for a diagnosis, Nurse Ratched popped her head back into the cubicle.

"Hey, one of my co-workers said they recognized you from that Greek movie. Were you in it? The aunt? 'What do you mean you don't like meat, I'll make you some lamb?' Is that you?"

"Yes," I replied weakly as I held on to my arm, "that's me."

"Hey, Bob," she shouted, "it *is* her."

Three other nurses were now standing in my room, staring and laughing.

"You were funny."

"Are you still acting?" one of the nurses asked. "I don't see you in anything anymore."

I held up my arm, which now looked like the offspring of a Goodyear blimp and an eggplant.

"Yes, I'm still acting, and will the swelling go down?" I asked.

"Probably. If it doesn't, see a doctor."

"Hey, what was Nia Vardalos like? My father's friend knows someone who knows her."

"She was lovely," I said. "Sorry, I don't mean to change the subject, but I'm not having a stroke, am I?"

Before they could answer, the doctor appeared with my chart. "Ms. Martin. Now I know who you are. I've been racking my brain to figure it out. *SCTV*?"

"That's correct, doctor."

"I haven't seen you in anything lately. Are you retired?"

"Yes," I said, lying, determined to put an end to the career interrogation and get to the important matters at hand, like my death.

"Doctor, are my symptoms serious? Do you think it's my heart?"

"No, all the tests came back negative. You had a bad case of indigestion. Gastroesophageal reflux. But you were smart to come to emergency. The symptoms are often confused. You're fine to go. By the way, Catherine O'Hara and my wife went to high school together. She's so talented. She's *always* working."

The next day, back on the set of my TV series, my swollen arm and bruises were camouflaged under makeup and a long-sleeved shirt. When the crew and cast asked me if I was okay, I told them I had been diagnosed with "indigestion." Believe me, I would rather have used the more glamorous and exotic term "gastroesophageal reflux," but who the hell can pronounce *that* name either. Oh, to be twelve years old again, with the *mumps*.

Multi-Tasking

I am in a double banger right now. That's show-biz talk for a trailer/Winnebago that acts as a dressing room for actors while they are shooting on location. Each banger, divided by a wall, houses one actor. Double banger, two actors. Triple banger, three actors.

A banger is a cozy little cubicle (on wheels) with windows and comes complete with microwave, refrigerator, sink, small couch attached to the wall, toilet that you flush by pushing a pedal, plastic-encased shower, and table with a large mirror and makeup lights surrounding it. It's not a bad place to spend an hour, but hair-pullingly claustrophobic if you're forced to stay in it any longer. It's a little roomier than the hole in which Saddam Hussein was found, but only slightly.

Years ago, I shared a double banger with another actress. After she ate anything, she desperately tried to work off the calories by jogging in place in her banger, simultaneously shaking mine. Bangers have thin walls. You don't want to confide anything to anyone while you're in your banger, let alone have sex.

That's another experience I had in a banger while shooting a low-budget made-for-television movie in the '80s. I shared a double banger with an actress who was dating a big movie star. He was married to someone else. That didn't stop them from having clandestine lunchtime sex in her banger, twice a week. The banger would vibrate, and I would be forced to eavesdrop on their explicit sexual encounters. It was like listening to an episode of *Homeland*. Banging in a banger. One step up from banging in a car. Two steps up from banging in an airplane washroom.

All of those locations have their advantages, and all are dangerous and steamy. I've enjoyed sex in two of the aforementioned locations in my life, but having sex in a banger is something I've yet to cross off my bucket list. My lunch breaks on film sets, so far, have consisted mainly of devouring barbecued ribs from catering and taking a food-induced nap.

I am a guest star today on *30 Rock*, the NBC sitcom written by and starring Tina Fey. We are somewhere in Queens, though I don't know where. And it doesn't matter. Everything I need is in a one-block radius: my trailer, the makeup trailer, the wardrobe trailer, the set, and most importantly, the craft services table ("crafty," it's called).

Crafty is a little cordoned-off section near the set where you can find coffee, water, candy, cookies, nuts, granola bars, fruit, bread, peanut butter and jelly, and more candy, at all hours of the day. We are on location because the scene I am shooting calls for a banquet hall, and the *30 Rock* studio, where the show is usually shot, is too small a space.

I am thrilled to finally get to work with Tina Fey. Both of us began our careers with Second City, albeit twenty years apart, and I have been a great fan of hers since watching her on *Saturday Night Live*. Every word in this script, from start to finish, is hilarious. This is *30 Rock*'s last season. In fact, it has one more month to shoot before its ends its seven years on the air.

In 2006, while I was appearing in *Young Frankenstein* on Broadway, I was offered the part of Tina Fey's mother on the show. I had to decline because we were in previews and I couldn't get off the necessary shoot days from the musical. I was, of course, disappointed. Over the years, I had hoped there might be another opportunity to do the show, but one never materialized until last week, when I was offered this hysterical part of Bonnie Badamath (think *bad at math*), the chairperson at an awards ceremony and women's event called 80 Under 80, Celebrating Women in Media.

Liz Lemon, Tina's character, is receiving the top award, but Bonnie is less concerned with Liz's award and more concerned about her husband, Gary, who has recently ditched her to marry their realtor, who was in the process of selling Gary and Bonnie their dream house.

"I miss Gary so much," Bonnie cries out. "I put his sweater on a body pillow and took it for a canoe ride."

It's not a big part but it's funny, and I love being on camera interacting with Tina and Jane Krakowski, and taking direction from the brilliant writers and director.

I have been on many sets in my career, and usually pass the time, when I'm not needed in the scene, obsessively going over my lines and making return trips to crafty. I have never learned to use my time productively while shooting a film or TV show and have always marvelled at actors who can. But that requires multi-tasking, and it's not something that comes easily to me or, by the way, at all.

Many years ago I was a guest along with Steve Martin on Marty Short's sitcom. Steve would finish a scene on camera and then return to his trailer (*Mr.* Martin did not have to share a double or triple banger; he had a *trailer* all to himself) to continue writing his movie script, or his novel, or his play. It didn't matter the genre because the point is he was multi-tasking. I'd be eating my fifth doughnut while he was completing the first act of an award-winning something. One of my favourite people, Seth Rudetsky, my musical director and a writer, actor, and popular radio personality, can be playing the piano, reading a book, and finishing his weekly column for *Playbill* all at the same time. It is so annoying and distracting to be on stage with him during rehearsals and watch him read his book as I'm trying to remember my lines, and yet, on cue, he'll put the book down and start accompanying me. I am so envious at his multi-tasking abilities.

So today I am experimenting. I brought my computer with me, and between takes and during lunch, in my banger, I'm going to write an essay for my book. This experiment is fraught with anxiety. What if I forget my lines because I won't be going over them repeatedly? What if I get into another mindset, that of a writer, and can't make the switch back to actor? What if I don't return to the craft services table in five minutes and all the Twizzlers are gone? I guess you could say I'm doing a little cognitive behavioural therapy on myself. I'm trying to contain the anxiety that comes up when I am not doing the same compulsive thing I've always done. It seems to be working right now, until I think about the lines I have to say in the next scene, and worry that if I don't repeat them ten times in a row, I'll forget them when I get in front of the camera. If this exercise works today, and I write an essay *and* remember my lines, I will feel enormously empowered. I will go on talk shows and be lauded as the woman who rewired her brain over lunch and finished her book.

For every Broadway show in which I have ever appeared, whether it's a one-night-only performance or daily performances during a twelve-month run, I go over all my lines before I go on. I say them out loud, in my dressing room, in the wings, and right before I make my entrance. The brilliantly funny and confident actress Megan Mullally and I appeared in *Young Frankenstein* on Broadway together. One night before the start of the show, Megan came into my dressing room. We chatted a bit and then, slightly panicked, I announced that she had to leave because I had to prepare.

"Prepare what?" she asked.

"I have to get into character and go over my lines," I said.

"You do?" She kindly left my dressing room, but I could hear her laughing all the way back to hers. After all, we were in our fifth month of the run. It was preposterous to think I still had to go over the lines.

Noise distractions are a big culprit in keeping me from staying focused. I never knew that sound sensitivity had a name, but it turns out it does: misophonia. I just read about this newly discovered disorder in the *New York Times*. Misophonia is the hatred of specific sounds—not loud noises, but small irritating noises: someone breathing or clearing his throat, water dripping. It's something I've lived with for years. Someone chewing gum, someone sniffing, the TV on really softly, a goose quacking in

the distance, someone clicking a pen, Alicia Keys singing at any volume, anywhere, is enough to make me lose
it. The other day I was on a plane and the guy two rows
over was turning pages in a magazine aggressively (as I
was trying to read a book), and the sound of the pages
flipping unravelled me. I had to put my book down and
put my hands over my ears as I proceeded to stare him
down. He was completely oblivious that his page-turning
was turning me into a killer. My mother always snapped
her chewing gum, and it felt to me like the sound of someone writing on a chalkboard. My best friend, Deb Monk,
was chewing gum when I first met her. I asked her to spit
it out, and because she is so loving, she did. In fact, she
always spits out her gum when she sees me because she
knows my triggers. She is a true friend.

Now that I have a name for my extreme intolerance of certain noises—misophonia—I feel special and legitimate. I read
that Kelly Ripa also suffers with misophonia. I wish it was Liv
Ullmann who had this infliction. I would then be included
in an elite artistic circle of fabulously sensitive Norwegian/
Armenian actresses. Anyway, there's comfort knowing I'm
not alone.

By forcing myself to do an activity that is not routine—
writing, for instance, when I ordinarily would be going

over my lines—I am also slowing down any age-related mental decline. Writing in my banger is a neurobic exercise. Neurobics involve using your senses (sight, touch, smell, hearing, taste) differently from how you normally would. Neurobic exercises activate brain cell activity. Change is good, and healthy for your brain!

Other examples of neurobic activities:

> Eating with your non-dominant hand.
> Brushing your teeth with your non-dominant hand.
> Using the Braille numbers in the elevator and at the ATM.
> Taking a completely different route to work.
> Learning and using sign language.
> Rearranging where you put your cosmetics.

I'm willing to try anything that will extend my life, except sorting out my cosmetics. Seriously, I can't throw away any of my makeup. Eyebrow pencils, concealers, lipstick, rouge—that's how long I keep makeup. No one even uses the word "rouge" anymore. I have tubes of lipstick I bought in the '60s, my favourite being Cherries in the Snow by Revlon. They still make that colour, by the way, and I keep buying new lipsticks of the same shade, but I can't throw away the half-used original tubes. I might be the only actress alive who still has a stash of Max Factor's Clown White. And

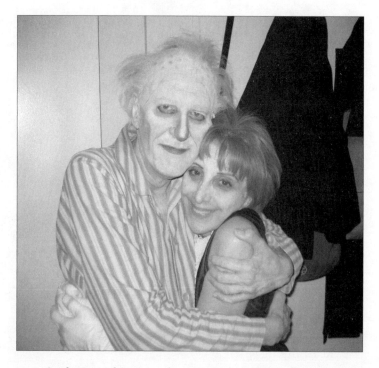

amazingly, I used it recently, on stage with Geoffrey Rush in Broadway's *Exit the King.*

You never know when you'll need clown white. And unlike milk, makeup doesn't turn after ten days. It seems to have a shelf life of at least fifty years.

But back to neurobics and how to rewire my brain.

Next week, I start French lessons.

Today, I am going to drink my Starbucks coffee with my non-dominant hand.

And tomorrow I'll take a different route to work.

I will reconfigure my brain, without drugs, without

therapy. I will live till I'm one hundred. But if someone doesn't fix that fucking faucet in my bathroom, I'm going to rip it out of the wall.

Squirrels

Yesterday I hired an animal control company to remove a squirrel's nest outside my home. The mother squirrel had dragged branches and leaves from my willow tree into an eavestrough beneath my bedroom window. Of course, I knew none of the specifics, like who dragged what where, until Jaime, the wildlife removal expert, confirmed what kind of animal it was. I was thinking possibly raccoon, but that didn't entirely make sense. A raccoon is much bigger than an eavestrough, and yet how could a small squirrel gnaw off branches from a willow tree and drag them a few feet to the gutter? Jaime took a look from the yard and in one instant yelled out, "Squirrels, and believe me, I've got no problem slapping that squirrel's head around."

"Isn't that dangerous? Won't she attack you?" I asked, completely ignoring the fact he planned to punch out the little guy and make mince-rodent out of her.

He replied, "Squirrels ain't the brightest animals. Once I slap his face around a little bit, he knows who's boss and he won't come back."

Jaime walked into my bedroom and climbed out the window onto the roof. As he approached the nest, an adult squirrel frantically jumped out of it and onto the adjacent tree. Jaime then put on some gloves and continued with glee and maniacal anticipation to dismantle the nest. Meanwhile, the squirrel, perched on her tree branch, was watching nervously. Jaime took full advantage of the onlooking squirrel. He dislodged one branch at a time and crumbled it in front of the now homeless rodent. He cackled and taunted the squirrel by shaking each branch in front of her. Jaime was the alpha. He was showing the squirrel who was in charge.

Suddenly Jaime stopped and quizzically looked into the nest.

"What's that high-pitched squealing?" I asked. "Do you hear that?"

"Babies," Jaime replied.

"How many?" I asked nervously.

"Probably three to five," he confidently responded.

He took off his gloves, stuck his hand in the nest, and gently removed the first baby. It was pink, about three inches long, and had arms and legs and a suggestion of a tail. Its eyes were not yet open, but it was squealing and squirming in Jaime's palm.

Jaime stuck his hand back into the nest and one by one pulled out three more babies.

He then took out his iPhone.

"Do you have a dish or a box?" he asked.

"Of course." I ran down to the kitchen and picked out an aluminum pie plate. (Was that an unconscious act? Was I thinking of squirrel pie?)

I brought the plate back to Jaime. He placed it on the roof and put the four babies into it, then clicked on his iPhone camera. I glanced at the tree and saw that the mother had vanished.

"What are you doing, Jaime?" I asked, feeling unsettled as I stared at the four pink squirrel newborns squirming in the pie pan.

"I'm making a movie. The mother will be back in a minute to get the babies, and I want to film this."

Good, I thought. The mother squirrel had bolted when Jaime initially approached the nest. How could a mother, in spite of the presence of an evil giant looming over her nest, leave her defenceless babies, not more than a few days old? My maternal instincts were on fire. As a member of Million Moms for Squirrels, it was my duty to stand up for these helpless babies, these newborn and not particularly attractive vermin.

Jaime and I waited for the mother squirrel to return. She was nowhere in sight.

"Oh my God, Jaime, the babies are in an aluminum pie

plate. Will they roast in the sun? Should we take them out? What if the mother doesn't come back right away?"

"She'll be back. Trust me."

Jaime placed the plate out of the sun, in the corner of the roof, and climbed back into my bedroom. I grabbed an empty shoebox, climbed out onto the roof, and positioned the box over the plate in such a way that the babies wouldn't suffocate and would still be seen from the window. The babies were now protected from the sun, though not protected from other potential killers: raccoons, herons, and seagulls—not to mention the elements, rain and wind.

"She'll be back. Trust me."

It was time for Jaime to move on to his next appointment. His work as the squirrel exterminator was done. I wrote a cheque for $333.35 and handed it to him as he got in his truck.

"Jaime," I asked. "Did we do the right thing? If we hadn't dismantled the nest, would the squirrels have moved on after they became stronger?"

"You did the right thing," Jaime said. "They would have made a home there and eventually dug their way into the attic. Toronto has thousands of squirrels. Don't feel bad."

The pied piper of the GTA smiled reassuringly and drove away.

I did feel bad. And guilty. I kept checking throughout the day to see if the mother squirrel had come back to

retrieve her young. I thought of bringing the babies into
the house and feeding them with an eyedropper and raising them as pets.

They wouldn't have been my first pet rodents.

When my sons were small, we had a pet rat named Cocoa.
We loved the little guy. He was smart and cute and cuddly.
His home was a cage in the kitchen, but often we would let
him out to play. He greeted my sons at the front door when
they came home from school. He sat on my sons' shoulders
as they did their homework. He could find his way out of
a maze that my sons built from blocks. Cocoa lived almost
three years, unheard of for a pet rat, whose usual life span is
two years. He developed a skin rash that took over his body,
and eventually his hind legs became paralyzed. Even though
I purchased Cocoa for $2, I spent over $500 on medicine
and visits to the veterinarian to keep him alive. When I drove
Cocoa away in his cage to be put down, my sons and I cried.
Cocoa was a grey rat that looked like he'd been plucked from
the tracks of the A train in Manhattan, but we loved him.

I have known other people to raise pet rats, but I have
never heard of a pet squirrel, which is kind of interesting,
really, when you think that the nickname for a squirrel is "a
rat with a tail."

But now my sons were grown and I'd be nursing four
squirrels back to health, only to wreak havoc in my home and
nest inside my five-hundred-count Egyptian bedding. And I
had better things to do with my time than build a maze out

of blocks on the floor. That's not entirely true. I have plenty of time to build a maze, anywhere, but it seems like a lonely, crazy thing for a sixty-five-year-old woman to do on her own. I would, however, have taken the time to train them to greet me at the door. That would have been charming.

Still, I couldn't stop thinking of the babies.

By the evening, five hours later, it started to rain. The temperature was dropping and there was no sign of the mother. I went to bed and prayed all night that the babies would be gone when I woke up. Not eaten by a raccoon but lovingly rescued by their guilt-ridden mom.

At 5:30 a.m., I gingerly opened the bedroom curtains. One baby had managed to escape, or the rain had washed him out onto the roof. He lay dead a few feet away. The three other babies, all huddled together, were dead in the pan. I was heartsick.

Did I kill them? Was I their surrogate mom and I let them die?

I remembered a book I read to my children when they were little. It was called *Are You My Mother?*

I could never get through the book without falling apart. In the story, a baby bird hatches from his mother's egg, just after the mother bird leaves to find food for her baby. The baby does not see his mother anywhere. And so he goes to look for her. He can't fly, so he walks and walks, looking for his mother. He asks a kitten, a hen, a dog, and a cow if they are his mother. They all reply no. The baby bird eventually is dropped back into its nest by a crane and is reunited with its mom. I bought a copy of the book recently to give to a new mother, and as I reread it in the bookstore, I began to cry uncontrollably.

What's behind this unbridled show of emotion toward a fictional motherless bird in a book, and four dead baby squirrels on my roof?

Why can I cry at this sight and be torn apart, yet not feel gut-wrenching despair at the carnage in Syria, the murder of twelve moviegoers in Colorado, young soldiers dying in combat all around the world? How can these tragedies not touch my heart, make me want to do something to change these heinous crimes against humanity?

I am so desensitized by images on TV, by self-serving newscasters, by exploitative websites, that very little out there touches my heart. I want to feel in my bones the atrocities committed every day. But I feel nothing. Instead, I glance at the latest headline, shake my head in sorrow for a moment, and carry on with my life, my very comfortable life. Nothing really penetrates for long.

Too much pain. Too much sadness to let in. I cry over a dead two-day-old squirrel but not for twelve innocent people who died by an insane boy's rifle in Aurora.

I can touch the baby squirrel. Cradle it. Bury it. Be its mother.

I turn off the TV, crumple up the newspaper, and go about my day.

My Pine Tree

I hear the chainsaw. I can't look outside. I'm frozen at my desk. Two men are on my terrace, where my pine tree has sat for the last forty years. They have been ordered to cut down the tree.

The Latin name for my pine tree is *Pinus bungeana*, a rare, beautiful Chinese pine. A lacebark pine, it is called, because of the delicate lace design on the bark.

It had lived for more than forty years on my terrace, and that is no small feat. My apartment in New York is on the seventeenth floor. It's a penthouse apartment with a huge wraparound terrace. Last week, I received a certified letter from the landlord's lawyers demanding that the tree be taken off the terrace because the weight was causing damage to the roof. There was no way to lift it and get it into the elevator. By now, it was more than twelve feet high. There was no way to dispose of the tree other than to chainsaw it apart.

Back in 1979, when I moved into the apartment, I discovered that the previous tenants had left the tree behind. It was small then, a few feet high, secure in its terracotta pot. It was indestructible. It kept flourishing against all odds. Over the years, I had containers especially constructed for it. It cost me thousands of dollars to have them hand-built and assembled, and the tree planted and replanted and repotted. Nothing deterred this tree from growing; it has survived brutal winters, high blustery winds, ice, snow, pollution, bugs, lack of rain, too much rain. Occasionally, because of fifty-mile-an-hour winds, it has toppled over, been lifted back up, and kept thriving. It's been tethered to the railing that sits perched upon the parapet that wraps around my terrace. Or more precisely, *their* terrace. The landlord reminds me every time I let the pronoun "my" slip out unconsciously. I don't own the apartment. I rent it.

I first rented it almost forty years ago, with my closest friend, Claude Tessier. My darling, dear Canadian boyfriend. Claude was a dancer and singer, and spoke with the slightest French-Canadian accent. He was born in Hull, Quebec. We met in Prince Edward Island in a production of *Anne of Green Gables*, and we instantly bonded. We dated and then lived together back in Toronto. Claude was bisexual and, eventually, as painful as the realization was for our relationship, he made the decision to be exclusively with men. We kept our deep friendship and co-signed the lease to our apartment in 1976.

By then Claude was working on Broadway. He had been snatched up in Toronto by Broadway producers and given a work permit to appear in *A Chorus Line*. He was cast as an understudy in the original production. He was the go-to boy for understudying. He learned quickly, was reliable, never missed a step, a line, a verse. I saw *A Chorus Line* fourteen times while Claude was in it. I was always so proud to sit in the audience and witness my exceptionally talented best friend shine on stage.

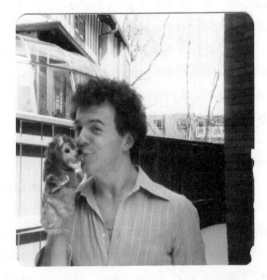

I married Claude in the spring of 1979 so that he could get a green card. That way, he wouldn't have to worry about being deported. Claude moved from show to show. *Copperfield, Cats, Evita,* and *Les Misérables.* I don't ever remember him being out of work. Everyone loved Claude, but I loved him more than anyone. He was my soulmate.

We were perfect roommates. I worshipped him, and we were devoted to each other. Claude loved taking care of me. He cooked for us and decorated the apartment. He macraméd, knit, played the recorder, the piano; his tap shoes, always worn out, crowded the closets. He picked audition songs for me, cheered me up with hand puppets he had made, taught me how to tap, and even picked out my wedding dress when I later married Bob Dolman. He witnessed the birth of my two sons, and they loved him.

Claude was on the road, in Florida, touring with *Les Miz*. He called me in Los Angeles where I was then living, and told me he was very sick. This was the late '80s, when there were murmurs of a "gay" disease called AIDS, but I didn't know anyone who had it yet. And then Claude started showing the symptoms. He was tired. He had constant diarrhea. He was weak. He couldn't continue with the show; the production was flying him back to New York.

Claude's dream for me was that one day I would star on Broadway. I had all but given up the dream for myself. I had two small children and was deeply ensconced in my life in Pacific Palisades, California. And then out of the blue I got a phone call to audition for *My Favorite Year*, a new musical by Lynn Ahrens and Stephen Flaherty that was being adapted for Broadway from the successful movie starring Peter O'Toole. It was 1989. I was asked to fly to New York to audition. I didn't want to leave my kids. But Claude encouraged me to audition. I knew how important it was to him. I got the part. It was my first role on Broadway. Claude was forty and I was forty-four.

The truth is, the real reason I left my two small children with their dad in Los Angeles was to be with Claude as he tried to fight his dreadful disease. I didn't want him to be alone. I wanted to take care of him. We lived together once again. By then he was very sick. Claude was extremely thin, losing weight rapidly. He had sores all over his face, cold sores on his lips, and reddish-purple marks everywhere else on his body. He was weak and so frightened of being alone.

"Please, can I sleep with you tonight, Andrea? I'm scared," he said.

"Yes, my darling, come into bed."

We shared the same bed for weeks while I was in rehearsals, until previews started. I wasn't sleeping, and I was exhausted. It was becoming too difficult to take care of Claude. His behaviour was erratic. Hallucinating, he'd pack his bags and say that he was flying to Florida for a vacation. "Come back, honey," I would say to him as he struggled, one unsteady step at a time, to walk to the elevator. "Come back, let's unpack your bags and I'll run you a bath, and you can put your pyjamas on and get all cozy and comfortable in bed, and I'll sit with you and read you a story. Doesn't that sound like a nice thing to do, honey?"

"Okay, I'll go to Florida tomorrow."

"Yes, darling. Tomorrow. But for now, let me take your bags, and you sit and I'll run you a bath."

While my show was still in previews, Claude was admitted to Lenox Hill Hospital. The dear, kind nurses there on the eighth floor, the AIDS floor, looked after him. Every day before rehearsal started, I would visit Claude, and every night after the curtain came down, I would run to Lenox Hill to be with him again. "Hang on, Claude, please hang on," I'd say. "It's our dream, honey. Both of us on Broadway. What you always wanted. What I always wanted. I want you in the audience on opening night. I need you in the audience. I want to make you proud."

Claude died during a preview performance, three days before opening night. The stage manager met me in the wings and told me the hospital had called and that Claude had passed away. The show was not the hit we all hoped it would be, but six months after we opened, I won the Tony Award for Best Featured Actress in a Musical. Our Tony Award, Claude's and mine. It was his last gift to me. I know this.

And now our pine tree is being sawed in half. It is killing me. Claude's and my tall, beautiful pine tree, which witnessed our life together. It's the end of an era. I can't bear to go out there and see what they have done to our tree. The sound of the saw is cutting a hole in my heart. I have never emptied the one closet that still holds most of Claude's mementoes from Broadway. His gold *Chorus Line* top hat, his tap shoes, the original sheet music from *Les Miz*, his pens and colouring pencils and sketch pads and handmade puppets, and headshots and recorder and resumés and signed photo from Michael Bennett, the director and choreographer of the Broadway cast of *A Chorus Line*—I have never been able to part with any of these things. Our pine tree was a witness to the deep bond and love I had for this man. Now it's gone. There are no more witnesses. Just memories.

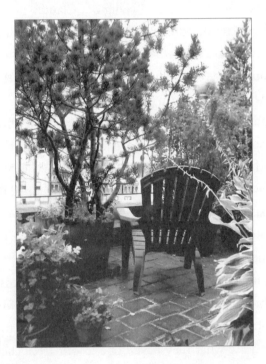

The Train

I'm on the train now, in the quiet car, travelling from Penn Station, New York City, to Wilmington, Delaware, where I will be performing my one-woman show for the next week.

The gentle motion of the train, the gentle passing by of the trees and houses and tracks and streams and backyards and discarded cars, makes me think of death in Venice. Not my death, although it would be romantic to die in Venice in the arms of a gondolier. No, I'm thinking of someone else's death in Venice. I guess I'm thinking of the movie and the last sad image of the boy sitting alone in the café. Or maybe there was no boy, and no café. My memory is shaky. But the passing images feel cinematic. Flashing back in time to another era. Even though the seat I am in is plastic, and the passengers are dressed in shorts, T-shirts, and sandals, even though there are empty bags of potato chips and chyrons of train info above every doorway, even though the porter is surly and his uniform is dirty and too small for him, even though the café car serves cold pizza and packaged fast food, I still think the train is romantic and I wish I were on my way to Venice. Not to die. But to locate the hotel I might die in, when the time is right.

My Lost Youth

It's so fitting. It's rainy and dark outside. There was a thunderstorm at 6 a.m. It woke me up from my sleep at the Portland Harbor Hotel. I had spent the last night in Portland, Maine, where I had dinner with my brother and his wife. I stayed at the hotel in order to get an early train to Boston this morning. The train from Portland to Boston has been operating for only ten years. As the taxi drove up to the station, I thought back on my childhood growing up in Portland and realized I had never seen a train station here before. I think there must have been one years ago. All cities were accessible by trains at one time, weren't they? There's so much about my childhood that I don't remember.

While I was waiting for the taxi, I sat in the lobby of the hotel and picked up a book on the history of Portland. It was lying invitingly on the table next to my wingback chair.

And there it was, on the first page, the beautiful poem by the New England poet Henry Wadsworth Longfellow:

My Lost Youth
Often I think of the beautiful town
  That is seated by the sea;
Often in thought go up and down
The pleasant streets of that dear old town,
  And my youth comes back to me.
    And a verse of a Lapland song
    Is haunting my memory still:
    "A boy's will is the wind's will,
And the thoughts of youth are long, long thoughts." . . .

And Deering's woods are fresh and fair,
  And with joy that is almost pain
My heart goes back to wander there,
And among the dreams of the days that were
  I find my lost youth again.
    And the strange and beautiful song,
    The groves are repeating it still:
    "A boy's will is the wind's will,
And the thoughts of youth are long, long thoughts."

I am on the train now, on my way to visit my childhood best friend, Tina. She lives in Needham, Massachusetts. I am making the two-and-a-half-hour trip from Portland to

Boston, and have arranged for a car to pick me up at South Station to drive me another thirty minutes to Tina's home.

Tina was diagnosed eighteen months ago with glioblastoma, the most aggressive form of brain cancer. Her daughter, Jessa, wrote me a week ago that the tumour had spread and that Tina has been given six months or less to live. I have planned to spend the day with Tina and her daughter and son and four grandkids. The tumour has affected Tina's short-term memory and speech. I'm not sure how we will carry on a conversation. I'm not sure what Tina will remember about our past. But I am sure that when I see her, she will be smiling and giggling, and her arms will be outstretched, waiting to hug me, and she will say, as she always does when she sees me, "Oh, honey, honey. How are you, honey? I am so happy to see you."

This is an impossible journey for me. And yet, as I write this, I see how selfish that statement is—or maybe it's just human. What is the script I am going to follow when I visit with Tina for the next seven hours? What am I expecting to accomplish? Do we reminisce? Do I try to make her laugh and forget? Do I pretend that I will see her again? Another friend, having just lost a cousin who was diagnosed with pancreatic cancer, gave me this advice when I asked him how I should be, what I should or shouldn't say to Tina: "Be honest. Miracles do occur. You can tell her that you are going to cherish the present time together, while waiting for a miracle."

I'm not as brave as he thinks I am. I am scared. I am scared that I will fall apart and will not be able to be strong for Tina. I am scared that I will make the present worse for her, and that she will end up taking care of me.

Forty minutes before we reach Boston, I become nervous. Stage fright. That's what it feels like. Not sure of the role I'm playing. Not confident that I will remember my lines. Not even sure how I will inhabit my character. She'll see through it. I won't be convincing. I will be superficial and unable to stay present and in the moment. What am I so afraid of? That I won't be enough. That I will let my friend down. That I will be a fake. Tina, so authentic and genuine, someone so comfortable being who she is, deserves the same back from me.

Tina Stevens and I were best friends growing up together in Portland. "Tina" wasn't the name she was born with, but the only name I remember anyone ever calling her. Her real name was Mertina. Have you ever heard a name like that? I haven't. It's so original, like Tina herself.

Eighteen months ago, I received a phone call from Jessa, Tina's daughter. She said she and her mom were coming to New York for the day to consult with a neuro-oncologist because Tina's memory and speech were noticeably altered—something that had happened gradually over the past few weeks. It had been several years since I had seen

Tina. The last time we saw each other was when she came to see me on Broadway in *Young Frankenstein the Musical*. Whenever I appeared on Broadway, Tina would call to say she was bringing the family to New York. And then they would arrive, and I'd see how her granddaughters had grown, and we'd go out to dinner and reminisce, and then she'd load the whole family back in the car, and they'd make the trek back to Needham. Tina loved her grandchildren so much. Never said a judgmental word about anyone in her family. Just pure unconditional love. Tina had two children: Jessa, a physical therapist, and Josh, a paramedic and a registered nurse at a hospital in Needham. Although Jessa told me that both she and Josh suspected a brain tumour, they held out hope that it was benign. Tina had asked to see me. Jessa was calling because Tina's speech was difficult to understand, especially over the phone. But she wanted very much for us to get together. Of course, I said. We'll go out to dinner or we can order in, and then you'll spend the night with me. Whatever you need, please come. I would love to see you both. Secretly, I was scared at what I would see, and I could already feel the wheels of *How am I going to entertain her?* spin out of control.

If there was anyone I thought could fight this cruel disease, it was Tina. I have since learned she is losing the battle. I just received this email from her beautiful, loving children:

At this point, the doctor said that she has about two to six months left to live. And you may not be surprised to learn Tina is prepared to die. She is at peace with this, as Mom told Josh, Alecia, Greg, Hailey, Mackenzie, and Jessa when we all gathered together on Saturday night to share our love for each other and hear Mom tell us that she loves us all and is okay with what is happening.

It doesn't surprise me that Tina is at peace. She has always had deep faith. I envied her profound connection with the Church, and her life of service. That and her fierce independence. Never a victim, our Tina.

I don't know what to do with this devastating news other than write and keep writing until every memory between us has been reignited and I can believe, in some way, that I am prolonging her life.

I can hear Tina now. *Oh, honey, don't be silly. Please don't do that. Don't write about me. Write about yourself. Your life is so interesting. I am so proud of you. I am so proud of all you have accomplished.* And she would be laughing and giggling and asking me all about myself, and I would feel so damn important because that was just one of her gifts—making the other person feel so grand.

When we were growing up, I wanted so much to be like Tina. Petite and athletic, cute and confident. She was the head cheerleader at Deering High. I can see her so vividly in her purple-and-white uniform. Her short blonde hair cut in a bob. Her golden tanned face always smiling. Her hands clutching the pompoms that sat resting on her hips, her legs spread apart in a *V* as she stared directly into the bleachers, ready to shout out the next command.

"Sway to the left, sway to the right. Stand up, sit down, fight fight fight." So fitting a cheer for Tina. A fighter in the sweetest little package.

Tina and I were inseparable in high school. I tried so hard to be different and rebellious when I was growing up, in order to stand apart from everyone so I would be noticed, when all I really wanted was to belong. Tina, on the other hand, was a true free spirit. She didn't need to work hard at being someone she wasn't. She knew who she was. She was proud of who she was. She didn't make excuses for who she was. She didn't have to try to be anything.

One night—I was probably fourteen at the time—I was awoken by rocks being thrown at my bedroom window. I looked outside and there was Tina. It was 3 a.m. She had climbed up the tree next to the house and was now knocking on my second-story bedroom window. I opened it.

"Let's go to Dunkin' Donuts," she whispered.

Wow, what an adventure. How daring. How exciting. And Tina was going to lead the way. I just had to follow. I got dressed, snuck out the window, and both of us, in the middle of the night, walked the neighbourhood streets of Portland until we reached Dunkin' Donuts. We sat and ate doughnuts like big girls, and drank chocolate milk. We were not there long before we were approached by two policemen who had noticed two young, unaccompanied girls sitting in a doughnut shop in the middle of the night. This was Portland, Maine, in the early '60s. Believe me, we stood out. They put us in their patrol cars and drove us back home. I don't remember Tina being the least bit concerned. Why shouldn't we be able to get doughnuts at 3 a.m.? We weren't hurting anyone.

I was punished, of course. My mom, in her nightgown, answered the door and saw a policeman with her fourteen-year-old daughter, who she thought was upstairs asleep, and was speechless. Rebellious Andrea must have been the culprit who organized this dangerous outing. Sweet Tina got off without much reprimanding. I lost my privileges for a month.

Feisty. That is a perfect way to describe my friend. After high school, Tina went to nursing college. There she met her future husband, Jim, who was studying to be a doctor. After Tina's graduation, they moved to Manhattan, where Jim began his residency. I had just moved to New York, after graduating from college and touring with my first professional show, *You're a Good Man, Charlie Brown*. As I didn't yet have an apartment, Tina and Jim invited me to stay with them. Tina had recently given birth to a baby girl, Jessa. They lived on the Upper West Side in a high-rise apartment with the baby and a parrot she had found walking on Madison Avenue. Tina rescued the bird and brought him home. What was the parrot's name? Oh, I wish I could ask Tina right now. I wish I could pick up the phone and ask her. We have loved telling that story over the years. I fear she could not find the words now to tell me. Her speech is limited and her memory going.

I stayed with Jim and Tina on and off from 1969 to 1970. During that time, Jim was sent a draft notification. They had a new baby. He was in medical school. Tina didn't want Jim to be drafted. She did not want to lose her husband to the war. She took just enough pills to make it look like a suicide attempt so that Jim would be kept from going overseas. She was a nurse, after all, and she knew what she was doing. I thought it was the most brave and selfless act anyone could perform. She was singular in her devotion to the people she loved.

It is still grey and rainy and overcast and gloomy. The train's rocking motion is comforting, like the rocking of a baby in its mother's arms. It feels safe and nurturing and calming. And the past seems present and clear. All the many different memories are one. Our youth. Our lost youth. Tina's and my youth. Our lives. Our experiences. Our love for each other, one memory.

Thirty minutes to go to Boston. I have spent a good portion of my life running away. I can't today. I don't want to.

Tina, who kept me real during my youth, deserves me to be real today.

God give me the strength to be there for my friend so that our youth will endure. And Tina will remain alive forever.

Tina and I and her family spent the day together at her home in Needham. She knew who I was but never said my name. She told me over and over again that she loved me. We laughed and looked at old high school yearbooks, but I think that for most of the time she did not recall the people in the photos. A couple of times she recognized a face and I told her the name as she nodded in delight. Maybe it is a good thing that her memory is going rapidly. Maybe she does not realize that her death is imminent. She smiled from the time I arrived at 10 a.m. until I left at five that evening. She is nurturing and loving and will be a caring mother until her last breath. I did not say I would see her again. I cried, though I'm not sure she understood why. I told her I loved her over and over. When we went on a walk around her neighbourhood, away from her children, I asked her how she felt. She kept saying that her kids were happy. Nothing about herself. Just her kids. I sensed her increased frustration at her inability to communicate. I hugged her and said I was so grateful that we were together, that we should enjoy every moment in the present while we waited for a miracle. I think that she understood. She stopped and looked at me, and I felt, for that one moment that day, an unspoken acknowledgement between us of the truth.

That was the last time I saw Tina. The final image I have of her is her standing at the front door of her little house in Needham, with Josh and Jessa and the grandkids by her side. She was waving and smiling as I got in the taxi that would take me back to the train station. I kept looking at her as the taxi drove away. Tina never stopped waving and smiling until the car pulled out of sight.

Tina died a few weeks later, on September 14, 2012. Her daughter-in-law, Alecia, sent me this text:

Tina passed around 9 p.m., very peacefully and waiting until all four of her grandbabies were tucked into bed. We are happy she is whole again, but miss her already. Lots of love to you, her dear friend.

On December 2, 2012, Tina would have turned sixty-six years old. On that date I was performing in Boston, at the American Repertory Theater in the pre-Broadway tryout of *Pippin*. Tina's kids and grandkids were in the audience. The character I played in *Pippin* was Berthe, Pippin's grandmother. There is a lyric in the song "No Time at All" that Berthe sings:

I've known the fears of sixty-six years
I've had troubles and tears by the score.
But the only thing I'd trade them for
Is sixty-seven more.

That night I sang the song to Tina. I looked up into the rafters and imagined her there, waving and laughing.

Oh, honey. Oh, honey, sixty-seven more, she was saying. *You deserve that. I love you, honey. I love you.*

Part Five

My First Head Shots, Circa 1970

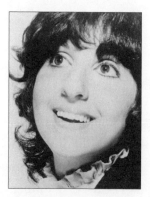

The Innocent Girl Next Door

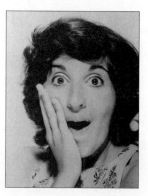

The Surprised Girl Next Door

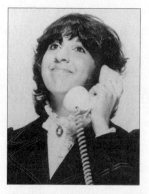

The Girl on the Phone Next Door

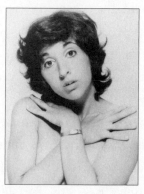

The Nude Girl with the
Medical Alert Bracelet Next Door*

*This last photo says, "I'm Hot, I'm Single, and I'm Allergic to Penicillin."

Yes!

I was asked to replace the renowned Canadian filmmaker Deepa Mehta, who was bedridden with the flu. She was to present the Best Canadian Film Award at the annual Toronto Film Critics Association (TFCA) gala dinner at the historic Carlu in downtown Toronto. On the day of the event, the organizers asked me to step in. Under usual circumstances, with such short notice I would have declined, if for no other reason than, with the holidays barely over, none of my clothes fit. And I *had* to look good at this event. Every Toronto film critic was going to be there. I did not want to give them ammunition to attack my fragile ego with disparaging remarks about my appearance. Many lauded Canadian directors would be present: Toronto's own David Cronenberg, and two hot Quebec filmmakers, Philippe Falardeau and Jean-Marc Vallée. I had to impress them. I was looking for work, after all, and would have killed to be in one of their magnificent films. Of course, I wanted to look my best. My insecurities about my body ran rampant. *Who was going to cast a bloated actor hungry for work? Why had I fed that hunger, over the holidays, with unlimited supplies of Timbits? Why were layers of doughnut grease still lodged in the crevices of my chin?* Also present would be press and photographers and television cameras. I certainly didn't need one more bad photo on Wireimage.com.

So I did what I always do when I have to make a decision. I called my sister, the voice of reason.

"Of course you have to do this. Don't be ridiculous. It's a good audience for you. Everyone thinks of you for television and stage. The film community needs to know you're still out there. It's great exposure. *Do* it."

Why was I being so neurotic about my appearance? As far as I knew, my looks had never gotten me a job before, even with the minimal cosmetic surgery I have had done. Yes, "conservative procedures" have been performed on me over the years to keep up with my youthful energy. At least, that was my rationalization. But to my knowledge, none of it led to more opportunity. All it did was force me to find more work, to pay off the cosmetic-procedure bills.

But back to the TFCA event. Once my sister convinced me to say yes, I started to write down some jokes, some material for the evening. Then it dawned on me. *What material? What the hell do I have in common with Toronto film critics? Why did they ask me to present an award?* I am so not part of the film community in Toronto. It would be like asking Conrad Black to host the Tonys.

Aside from Ivan Reitman's 1973 horror film *Cannibal Girls*, in which Eugene Levy and I starred, and in which I dined on Eugene's body parts at the end of the movie (more on that later); Bob Clark's 1974 sorority horror film *Black Christmas*, in which I, along with sorority sister Margot Kidder, were strangled by a psychopathic pervert who lived in the attic; and Mary Walsh's 2006 comedy *Young Triffie's Been Made Away With*, in which I played a crazy, drug-addicted wife of a drunk Newfoundland doctor, I had never appeared in another Canadian film.

It was 2012, however, the year I vowed to myself, to my agent, to my manager, and to my sister to say yes to everything that was offered to me. It was clear that, after a long career of saying no, I had to bravely start saying yes. The new me was committed to showing up, putting one foot ahead of the other, having fun, and letting go of the results. As Woody Allen said, 99 percent of success is just showing up. And with the insight of my astrologer, Althea, it became even more evident at my January 1, 2012, reading that it was time to change. She told me I had chosen a career path in which I was comfortable hovering *under* the radar of success. I had not allowed myself to climb to the top and stay there. It was time to believe in myself. She asked that every time I had an insecure thought, I draw a big X over the thought. It was time to stop thinking I had to please anyone but myself.

So, armed with positively aligned planets, I drew an *X* over my body thoughts, put on my loose-fitting short red party dress, glued on a couple of eyelashes, and started writing some jokes. Even though the organizers had told me that all I had to do was announce the nominees and the winners, they also added, "But feel free to crack some jokes." Cracking jokes does not come easily to me, contrary to what you may think. It takes work to come up with funny material without writers . . . in front of prospective employers. Okay, wait, now I was doing what I always do: worrying about what the audience may think. I just put an *X* over that thought. A medium-size *X*, but it was a beginning. I was going to follow in the footsteps of Ricky Gervais: extemporaneously ad lib brilliant remarks—*and* I would do it without help from a staff of writers. I was going to trust myself in the moment to come up with something hilarious and entertaining.

And by God, that's what I did. And it worked. I told a couple of the written jokes. I read a letter from Christopher Plummer, who couldn't be there. I read it like I thought Mr. Plummer would read it, overarticulating and emphasizing every sincere word on the page. I didn't do it to get a laugh. But it did. Now I was on an ad libbing roll.

I then read the names of the three best Canadian films of 2011 and their directors. Philippe Falardeau for *Monsieur Lazhar*, Jean-Marc Vallée for *Café de Flore*, and David Cronenberg for *A Dangerous Mind*. I was about to open the envelope and announce the winner when it was brought to my attention that I had said one of the titles incorrectly. *A Dangerous Method* was the name of David Cronenberg's film, not *A Dangerous Mind*.

"Oh dear," I gasped out loud. "I have made a terrible mistake and I apologize, Mr. Cronenberg. The name of your film is, of course, *A Dangerous Method*, not *A Dangerous Mind*. Now you will never cast me in one of your films." The audience laughed. "What can I do to repay you? I'll do anything. All night. Anything. Believe me, I'm sixty-five, time is running out, whatever you want." The audience was really laughing now. I realized I had let my age slip out, loudly, in an ad libbing moment of terror, over three mics and on camera, in front of every critic, every producer, and three of the most distinguished directors in Canadian film.

At that point, did any of the cosmetic work matter?

No, of course not. Here's what mattered. I said yes to life. Instead of staying home and watching a rerun of *Duck Dynasty*, I showed up. I was myself. I had fun. I had no expectations. I felt honoured to be a part of the TFCA Awards. Brian Johnson, the president of the TFCA, thanked me profusely for "stepping in and being the trooper I was." And he added, "You killed." Both Monsieur Falardeau and Monsieur Vallée introduced themselves to me and, independent of each other, said they were big fans. In their beautiful French-Canadian accents, they had me at "pardon." One of the most successful producers in Canada asked me to lunch to discuss ideas for a television show. I am booked to host another gala. I am booked to be a guest on three talk shows. I'm having coffee with a young writer about a film he has written, in which he would like me to play a part. Someone told me I had great legs. Two women came up to me and said they loved that I had said my age out loud. It was empowering for all us women, they exclaimed. I also found out that Mr. Cronenberg had been in the washroom during my faux pas and wasn't aware of anything I had said. I did not destroy my chances of being in one of his films.

No one commented on the Botox on my forehead, nor on the grease around my chin. No one said they thought I didn't belong at a Toronto film event. I hovered *over* the radar of success that night. And it felt good. Someone sent me a photo from the event. It was on Wireimage.com. I was standing next to David Cronenberg, who had his arm around me. I was smiling, and my red dress shimmered. I hope Deepa Mehta is over her flu, and that she's healthy. I'm grateful she gave me the opportunity to say *yes* at the start of a new year. It's going to be a good one for character actresses. I can feel it.

Old Lady Parts* #2

The other day I was combing theatre websites looking for my name—'cause what could be a more constructive use of time?—and I came across an article that began with *Andrea Martin has made a career out of playing old ladies.* At first I was mortified. How could anyone have pigeonholed me and my illustrious career so inaccurately? I then did a quick mental survey about the roles I had played on stage, and to my shock, the article was right.

In the '70s, when I was in my twenties, I was cast as, quite literally, the Old Lady in *Candide*, directed by Lotfi Mansouri at the Stratford Festival in Canada. On Broadway, I performed Aunt Eller in *Oklahoma!*, Golde in *Fiddler on the Roof*, Frau Blucher in *Young Frankenstein*, and yet again, the Old Lady in Hal Prince's *Candide* on Broadway.

*Really overused title.

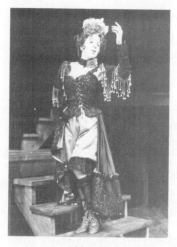

Old Lady

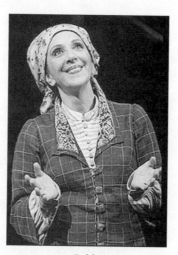

Golde

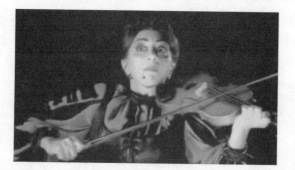

Frau Blücher

I played the part of Juliette, the old servant, in *Exit the King*; Dolly Levi in *The Matchmaker*; and an old drunk piano teacher in *On the Town*.

Yes, many roles I've played have been women older than me, but I don't think of them as old lady parts. I think of them as character parts. A character part is the sassy sidekick, the nosy neighbour, the town whore, the Jewish yenta—you get the point. I don't play the romantic lead who gets to make out with Ryan Gosling. I'm the house-keeper who walks in on them, does a spit take, trips over Mr. Gosling's underwear, and crawls on all fours out the door. (By the way, this movie hasn't been written yet, but I already hear that Betty White has beaten me out for the role.) I love playing character parts because you don't have to carry the show and you get all the great laughs.

Looking back, I realize it all started when I was a little kid. My first role ever was the Fairy Godmother in the Children's Theatre production of *Cinderella* in Portland, Maine. I was nine years old and already playing character parts.

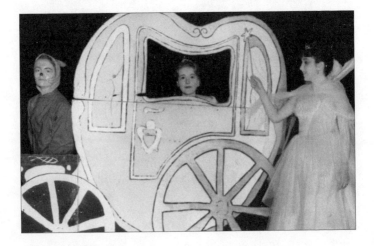

Thirty years later, I played another fairy godmother on *SCTV*, Mrs. Falbo.

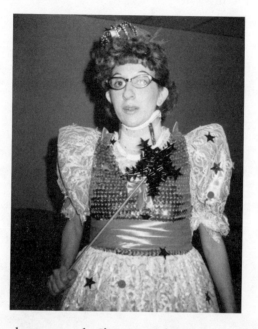

Every character role I've ever played has been rooted in my childhood: here I am as a forty-five-year-old Greek woman, Aunt Voula, in *My Big Fat Greek Wedding*.

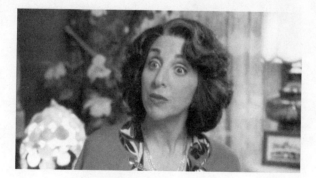

Here I am thirty-three years earlier at my high school prom, looking like a forty-five-year-old Greek woman.

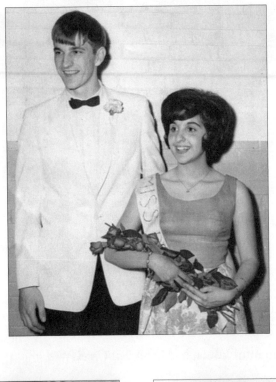

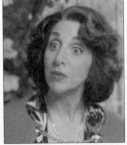

Forty-five year-old Greek woman

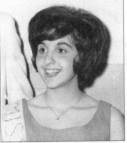

Forty-five year-old Greek woman

Lucy in *You're a Good Man, Charlie Brown* was my first professional character role.

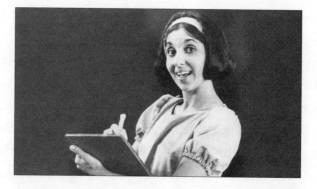

After that tour ended, I moved to Toronto, where I heard there were auditions for the Toronto premiere of *Godspell*. I had seen the show in New York and thought I'd be right for it, basically because it seemed that you didn't need to be a good singer or dancer to be in the show. It was a musical full of character actors with big personalities. I knew I was perfect for it. However, *they* did not. When I auditioned, hundreds of people were lined up to sing. I waited and waited, and finally my number was called. I got up onstage and, even though I knew the character description was "innocent follower of Christ," I did my signature audition song, "Somebody" from the rock musical *Celebration*, which would have been perfect for the live nude version of *Girls Gone Wild* but decidedly not for a Jesus disciple. I got halfway through, to just after the gyrating-hips section, and was then cut off abruptly. Some disembodied voice from the audience yelled, "Thank you, next"—three words no actor ever wants to hear, unless the words are immediately followed by "You got the part." I slunk back to my seat and continued to watch the auditions.

At that moment, I saw an adorable girl walk up on stage, with her hair in pigtails and her baggy trousers held up with brightly coloured suspenders. She skipped around the stage joyously and sang a childlike version of "Zip-a-Dee-Doo-Dah." She brought the house down. It was Gilda Radner. That was my cue to flee and walk directly to Dunkin' Donuts, where I bought and consumed a dozen crullers on my way to a Vic Tanny gym, where I then sat in the sauna for two weeks trying to sweat them off.

One day I heard my name over the loudspeaker; I was being called to the phone. I wrapped myself in a towel, walked to the phone in the locker room, and heard the distinctive voice of my friend Eugene Levy, who *had* been cast in *Godspell*. We knew each other from our award-winning performances as the stars of Ivan Reitman's *Cannibal Girls*. By "award-winning" I don't mean the Oscars, nor the Canadian Geminis. I mean at the Sitges. Anybody? It's the international fantasy and horror film festival. Yes, I indeed was in a horror film, made apparent by the poster that listed the title as *Cannibal Girls*, followed by the tagline "These girls eat men." Ivan Reitman was kind enough to cast us in one of his first films. Not the many huge hits that followed after. Nope. No room for us in *Meatballs* or *Ghostbusters*. But plenty of room for us to improvise the entire film of *Cannibal Girls*—"these girls eat men."

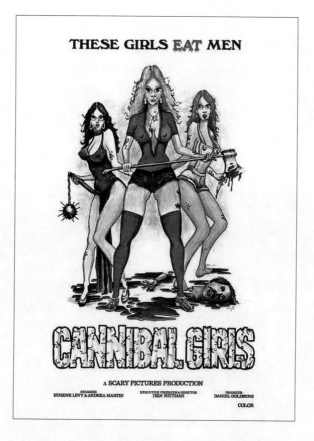

Eugene was calling to tell me that the girl who was cast to sing "Day by Day" was leaving the show. That night there was going to be a party for the entire cast, and he thought that if I showed up and was my wacky, character-y self, the director would see me and give me the job. I hung up and immediately put the canvas belt around my hips for a two-hour "workout" that consisted of the belt moving furiously around my lower body and giving me a skin rash but zero weight loss. But it didn't matter how I looked for *Godspell*. I showed up that night, cracked a few jokes, flashed ye olde perky tits, and got the part. It was the show that launched many careers: mine and those of Gilda, Eugene, Jayne Eastwood, Martin Short, Victor Garber, and our music director, Paul Shaffer. From that moment on, it was referred to as the Legendary Canadian Company of *Godspell*.

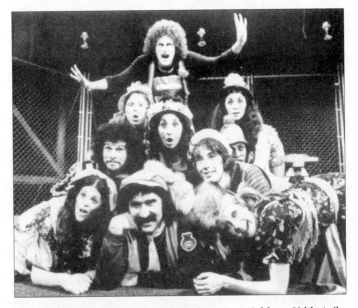

Clockwise from bottom left: Gilda Radner, Gerry Salsberg, Valda Aviks, Victor Garber, Avril Chown, Rudy Webb, Marty Short, Jayne Eastwood, and Eugene Levy, with me in the centre

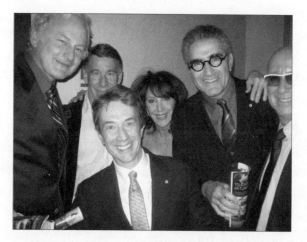

In the audience for opening night of the 2011 Broadway revival
of *Godspell. From left to right*: Victor Garber, Stephen Schwartz,
Marty Short, me, Eugene Levy, and Paul Shaffer

* * *

A dancer might dream of working with Bob Fosse or Michael
Bennett or Twyla Tharp; a screen actor, John Huston or
Martin Scorsese; but for a character actress/comedienne,
there's no one more idolized than Mel Brooks. I had the great
opportunity to work with Mel when he adapted his film *Young
Frankenstein* to the Broadway stage in 2007. Susan Stroman
directed Mel Brooks's *Young Frankenstein the Musical*, and I
was cast in the iconic role of the housekeeper Frau Blücher,
the role originally created in the movie by Cloris Leachman.

Mel loved improvisation. And, of course, my background
was in improv, but I was timid in front of him. While we
were in previews I wanted to change a couple of lines that

weren't working, and by that I mean, I wasn't getting the laughs I thought I could get. I sought advice from two of my friends, Marty Short and Nathan Lane, both of them having starred in Mel's previous and enormously successful musical *The Producers*. They both said, "Don't ask Mel if you can add a line. During a performance just do it, and if it gets a laugh, he'll let you keep it in."

So one night during previews in Seattle, we came to the scene at the castle where Frau Blücher (*Horse whinny.*) first meets Frederick von Frankenstein and his assistant, the voluptuous, buxom, sexy Inga. Think Pamela Anderson.

Frau Blücher is the first to speak.

FRAU BLÜCHER, *sounding ominous*: Good evening and velcome, Doctor Frankenstein. And who, may I ask, is this lovely young creature?
FREDERICK: She is my new laboratory assistant, Inga.
FRAU BLÜCHER: Assistant, huh? How do you do?

That's what was written. But that night, after I said "Assistant, huh?" I paused, looked at Inga, and added, "So that's vat they're calling them these days."

After a very long, exaggerated laugh, Frau Blücher continues. "How do you do?"

The audience roared. Mel came backstage after the show. He pointed at me and yelled, "It's in, but no credit!"

You know, it was one of those moments in my career that I took for granted, working with the one and only Mel Brooks.

I was caught up in the job and how to make Frau Blücher my own. Now when I look back on that time, I think of how fortunate I was to have worked with the comedy legend Mel Brooks, who now, in his eighties, still has the desire and the drive to make people laugh. He was opinionated and stubborn, but it was impossible to get angry with him. I remember when Anne Bancroft, Mel's wife of over thirty years, was interviewed by Charlie Rose, and he asked her what the secret of their long marriage was. She replied, "Oh, we've had our ups and downs like any couple, but every time I hear the key in the door, I know the party is about to start."

Mel sat in the audience every night for six weeks during our previews. He wrote a song for Frau Blücher, "He Vas My Boyfriend," and it was poignant and thrilling for me to perform it for him every night.

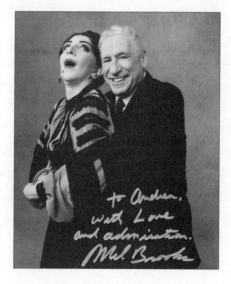

* * *

When I was offered the role of Berthe, Pippin's grandmother, a part originally played by Irene Ryan, who gained fame for her role as Granny on *The Beverly Hillbillies*, I adamantly said no. *Has it come to this?* I thought. *Now I'm being offered the part of a grandmother who makes her entrance in a wheelchair? My old lady/character parts have suddenly morphed into invalids? Forget it! Surely I have a few more years of middle-aged women roles left in me.* Right at the climax of a hysterical rant to my agent where I told him he might as well submit me for the revival of *Driving Miss Daisy*, I stopped in my tracks. My agent had interrupted me to inform me that the director Diane Paulus was going to collaborate with Les 7 doigts de la main, a circus troupe from Montreal. Suddenly everything changed, and I had an image of myself as the little clown Giulietta Masina in Fellini's *La Strada*, and not a dowager's-humped Miss Havisham in a bus and truck tour of *Great Expectations*.

I'd always had the fantasy of running away with the circus. Not the Cirque du Soleil version of circus but the darker side of circus, the freak-show version of circus, the Fellini version of circus where magic meets poignancy, where ugly meets spectacle, where mangled, extraordinary misfits with otherworldly gifts congregate, where there is no discrimination.

Who doesn't think of running away with the circus, metaphorically or literally?

It's the ancient heart of show business, the spirit of the travelling sideshow, older than vaudeville. Whenever I went to the circus, I had a religious feeling, like I was connecting to a tradition, to a long and flavoured dynasty. Elemental. Powerful. And I loved the weird spirit of the all-in view of entertainment. Animals, acrobats, freaks, clowns . . . nothing and no one was excluded from the circus. It was a beautiful, bountiful, generous view of the world.

I came close to running away with the circus in 1968. I was enrolled at Jacques Lecoq's École du Mime in Paris. This was the year of the student rebellion in Paris, of the assassinations of Martin Luther King and Robert Kennedy, but I was looking for my inner clown on the Avenue du Shtick.

I never completed the two-year course with Monsieur Lecoq. It was hard for me to be away from everyone I knew, so I returned home early and completed my speech/theatre degree at Emerson College, but I always regretted the decision of not finishing the course and sticking around long enough to see where that training might have taken me.

So before I passed on the *Pippin* offer, I asked my agent to set up a phone call with Diane Paulus, to hear how she planned on reimagining the show and what her take on Berthe was.

I then spent the afternoon listening to the *Pippin* score and, specifically, to the song "No Time at All." When Stephen Schwartz wrote that show-stopping number back in 1972, he was writing for the character of a sixty-six-year-old grandmother. But forty years ago, sixty-six looked very different from how it looks now. Life spans have increased—we are now living into our nineties, and sixty-six doesn't feel like the end of a life but the beginning of a third chapter.

The chorus of the song begins with the lyric "Oh, it's time to start living . . . "

In the original production, Berthe sings this to inspire the young Pippin as he searches to find meaning in his life. I had seen the show in my twenties and enjoyed the vaudevillian take Bob Fosse applied to the number. But the lyrics didn't have relevance to me then. Listening to them now as a sixty-six-year old woman, the line "it's time to start living" resonated deeply with me.

I went to bed that night and thought of Berthe as part of the circus troupe. The words that summed up the song to me were

> Here is a secret I never have told
> Maybe you'll understand why
> I believe if I refuse to grow old
> I can stay young till I die.

As I lay under the covers, I had a vision of Berthe as a young circus performer. Perhaps during her number the audience could see what she had been like in her prime—sometimes musicals have flashback scenes, with a second

actor playing the youthful version of a character, as in
Follies. Once again, I thought of Berthe's lyrics:

> I believe if I refuse to grow old
> I can stay young till I die.

Maybe I could be the sixty-six-year-old Berthe and also the
young Berthe in her prime?

The next day, Diane and I talked to each other for the
first time, on the phone, and within a few seconds of the
start of our conversation I began to excitedly rattle off
questions: "Why can't the character of Berthe be feisty and
sexy and agile and strong and determined and full of life,
all the attributes that I could bring to the table? Why should
we have to talk down to an audience and perform a clichéd
version of a grandmother? We have an opportunity with
the material to inspire women, not depress them. And if
every other character in your concept of *Pippin* is part of a
circus troupe, why can't Berthe also be a circus performer?"

Diane then introduced herself. I continued spewing out
my ideas. I told her I would be interested in taking the journey of her version of *Pippin* if she was open to Berthe performing a traditional circus routine in the show. I told her
I was willing to go to circus school so that the routine we
came up with would be authentic instead of a sight gag.

Diane was open to all my ideas, and I signed on for
the three-week pre-Broadway workshop at the American

Repertory Theater in Cambridge, Massachusetts, where Diane is the artistic director. The brilliant Gypsy Snider, one of the founders of Les 7 doigts de la main, was *Pippin*'s circus choreographer. She knew I wanted to do a circus routine and thought about it for about a week. One day she excitedly ran up to me. "I have the perfect routine for you! The trapeze!" she said.

"Wonderful!" I said. "Sign me on."

For the entire run of the show, at no point did she know, nor did I ever tell anyone, the following fact: I am *desperately* afraid of heights. Since being traumatized by my appearance in Harold Ramis's film *Club Paradise*, where I

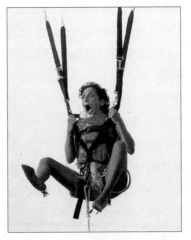

demanded to do my own stunt of parasailing, during which the rope that was tethered to the boat came unexpectedly undone and I was left drifting above the Atlantic Ocean, off the coast of Jamaica, where I waited for the wind to lower me somewhere that didn't, I prayed, have sharks, I have become a self-diagnosed acrophobe. Driving over bridges makes me anxious, hiking trails on steep mountains are no longer enjoyable, canopy rides in Costa Rica sent me screaming into the clouds, even looking over my terrace railing, which sits seventeen floors above Manhattan, makes me break out in a sweat.

But I was so determined to live out my fantasy of being a circus performer and, more importantly, to inspire the audience with Stephen Schwartz's life-affirming lyrics, that I was willing to put aside my fear.

I was told to show up at circus school in Brooklyn and meet my trainer one early morning. Even though I'd always worked out, it became startlingly clear as I tried the different apparatus that I had to completely change my body. Turns out, thirty minutes on the elliptical reading *Vanity Fair* three times a week doesn't help you when you have to hang twelve feet above a stage. I had to build my upper body strength and my core, at sixty-six years old. Not since *Rocky*. From then on, my workout regimen became daily weight lifting and cardio training in the gym, Pilates three times a week, and hot yoga. Plus I lowered my carb intake and cut out all gluten and dairy.

Yannick, one of the French acrobats in the cast, volunteered to be my partner. Gypsy methodically and patiently created a trapeze routine for us. We began with simple movements on the trapeze, low to the ground. Incrementally as I continued training with Yannick daily, I grew stronger, and the trapeze was slowly raised until we were floating twelve feet above the stage.

The *Pippin* workshop was a success. Diane Paulus's reimagining of the show was inspired brilliance. Two months later, we opened in Boston for a limited run to rave reviews and the show quickly transferred to Broadway.

We opened at the Music Box Theatre, in New York, on April 25, 2013, again to rave reviews, and for the next six months, eight times a week, Yannick and I performed our routine. And eight times a week, his hands became the only thing keeping me from plunging to my death. Every night as we were raised twelve feet above the stage on a rotating trapeze, my gorgeous twenty-five-year-old French partner looked into my eyes and quietly said in the most reassuring tone, "I will never let you fall. You can trust me." And I did. There was no net beneath us, no harness, no wires, and yet I was completely surrendered in his arms. There was no room for doubt as I lay suspended horizontally in mid-air, my body rigid in a plank position, my partner's fingers splayed across the outer edges of my firm belly as he held me beneath him while hanging by his knees on the trapeze. I looked graceful, relaxed, like a gliding bird, my arms outstretched, legs pressed tightly together behind me, my head held high as I stared into the audience with a smile on my face that reached the last row of the theatre.

Twenty years after winning my first Tony Award, I won my second for *Pippin*. When my name was called, I ran onstage and thanked all my collaborators—Stephen, Diane, Gypsy, and especially Yannick. I told the viewing audience, "I want to thank my partner, Yannick Thomas. *Merci, mon chéri, je t'adore.*" I continued, unconscious of the double entendre that slipped out of my mouth: "Do you know how wonderful it is for a woman of my age to be held in the arms of a man and not be dropped?" It was an unintended joke, but this portion of my acceptance speech was printed in media outlets across the country.

Over the run, friends and colleagues often came to my dressing room, and all of them asked the same question: "Aren't you scared on that trapeze?"

Each time, I said the same thing: "I'm aware when I'm up there that I have only two choices: to trust or to panic. I always choose trust. And then I'm not scared."

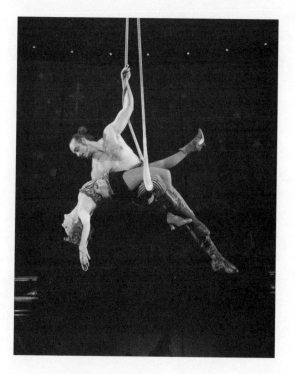

My last performance with *Pippin* was on September 22, 2013. For one last time, I took off the sexy, revealing corseted trapeze outfit that the gracious and inspired Dominique Lemieux had designed for me. I walked directly to Magnolia Bakery. Since then, I haven't stopped eating carbs, nor have I set foot in a gym. But oh, what a glorious year I had flying through the air with the greatest of ease.

The daring young character actress on the flying trapeze.

SCTV, or
"What Do You Think of This?"

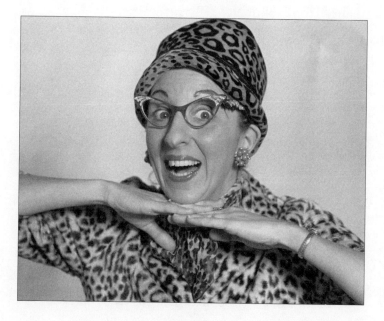

L adies and gentlemen, the past program director of *SCTV*,
Mrs. Edith Prickley.

"Hello, Canada and select cities in the USA. Edith Prickley here. And believe me, I don't want to be. *Pahaaaaaa!!!!!* I got better things to do than reminisce. I still have a whole drawer of underwear to wash and iron. But what was I supposed to do? I couldn't turn my back on an old friend. Andrea called me out of the blue this morning. Haven't heard hide nor hair from her in thirty years. There we were, Mr. Prickley and I, watching reruns of *Shark Tank* in our newly renovated ensuite at the Barrie Country Club and Retirement Village, when the phone rang.

"I thought it was those damn animal activists again. They cornered me in the parking lot at 7 a.m., just as my Zumba class was getting out. I was headed to kundalini practice when they started picketing my leopard outfit. They walked over to me and yelled, 'Edith, do you know how many animals had to die so you could wear that jacket?' and I said, 'Do you know how many animals I had to sleep with to get it?' *Pahaaaaaa!!!!!* At my age, I speak my mind.

"Well, it turns out, it wasn't those fanatics on the other end, it was a sad Armenian clown, and she was in a pickle. Saved her SCTV chapter for last and didn't know where to begin. She needed her memory jump-started and that's why she called me, yours truly, Mrs. P., to do her dirty work. Well, she called the wrong person. I don't remember a damn thing about my life or hers. I'm old. But personally, I don't give a rat's ass. I make up stuff all the time. And that's just what I told her to do. Who the hell's gonna know the difference? No one cares about the truth, they just want to know if John Candy was as nice a guy as he seemed. And he was. And if everyone got along. And they did. Fear will get you nowhere, Ms. Martin, so as my first husband, William Carlos Williams, said, 'Write what's in front of your nose.'

"And, while we're on the subject, let me tell you something about fear, folks. Fear is a redhead, capable of anything. Fear is the worst thing in the world, if you don't count audience participation.

These days I embrace everything about my life. And so does Mr. Prickley. He can't keep his horny hands off me. *Pahaaaaaa!!!!!* Why is everyone so afraid of getting older? Every time I get an invitation to join CARP, I fly into a violent rage. People think I look good for my age. That's some condescending bullshit—'You look good for your age.' You mean if I were younger and looked like this, you'd be rushing me to the emergency ward?

"I'm at that awkward age between retirement and a lovely coma.

"I'm so old, I still think Mel Gibson's a catch.

"I'm so old, macramé's starting to make sense to me.

"I'm so old, I remember when the Dead Sea was only sick.

"But that doesn't stop me. I keep on going. I say what I want and don't give a shit what anyone thinks."

"And so must you, Ms. Martin. Write whatever the hell comes to mind. Invent stuff. And then hire a lawyer."

* * *

Aw . . . Mrs. Edith Prickley. I love that broad. She's my alter ego. Who needs Pema Chödrön for enlightenment when you've got Edith Prickley by your side? She may not be a Buddhist nun, and she's loud and garish, but she's fearless. She imparts words of wisdom to the common man.

Mrs. Prickley has rescued me many times in my life. Just thinking of her makes me feel indomitable.

Edith was my go-to character for *SCTV*. When we were short on material, I'd get into my leopard outfit, stand in front of the camera, and spout off whatever came into my mind, on whatever subject was given to me. Not that everything that came out of my mouth was brilliantly funny, by any means, but audiences seemed to like Edith because she said what they wanted to say but couldn't. The '70s was a much more innocent time, and outrageously outspoken, off-colour comediennes were not as prevalent as they are today. Back then there was the trailblazing and incomparable Phyllis Diller, and her distant cousin, Mrs. Prickley.

Edith Prickley wasn't created during *SCTV*, however; she was created while I was performing with Second City in Toronto in 1977, at the Old Firehall theatre on Adelaide Street. And it is my darling and genius friend, Catherine O'Hara, to whom I credit Mrs. Prickley's birth.

The format of Second City has always been the same since its inception in Chicago in the '50s: a scripted segment is performed nightly, after which the improvisation begins—sketches based on audience suggestions. One evening, someone suggested we improvise a parent-teacher conference. The cast was backstage in the tiny shared dressing room, where we'd gather after the scripted segment was finished to wait for that night's list of suggestions. It was a grungy space in which males and females disrobed at the same time, and the air was permeated with the odour of stale cigarette smoke and booze. I was the only member of the cast who didn't smoke, and every night after the show I'd go home and shower for what seemed like hours to get the smell of smoke off my body and out of my hair. Irish coffee was the drink of choice backstage among the cast at Second City: hot coffee with Irish whiskey, topped with whipped cream and served in glass mugs. I don't know why that stands out in my memory, but it does. It's so vivid, my mental picture of Catherine, Eugene Levy, Dave Thomas, and especially Joe Flaherty and John Candy, standing by their cubicles, laughing and smoking and sipping hot toddies out of those dainty glass mugs.

Then we'd receive the list of audience suggestions, and the frenzy would begin. While the audience took an intermission, we had twenty minutes to decide which ideas we'd use for the second part of the show. Costumes and wigs and hats and props would be strewn about the room, everyone yelling out ideas and pulling clothes from the racks for scenes we were about to improvise for characters we were about to create.

Improv for me was both electrifying and terrifying. How I survived those nightly improvs is a total mystery. I really felt like a fish out of water. My performing experience before joining Second City had been scripted plays and musical theatre. But I loved the cast, and the excitement and challenge of being on stage nightly without a net outweighed my fear. And I was never ever bored. Improv kept me sharp *and* petrified. In the '70s, Second City was the only improvisational comedy institution around. Now improv is the fad. There's Upright Citizens Brigade, Chicago City Limits, The Groundlings, and, of course, Second City, which continues to produce some of the most gifted and successful comedians today. Tina Fey, Kristen Wiig, Maya Rudolph, Will Ferrell, Amy Poehler, Jane Lynch, Melissa McCarthy, Steve Carell, and Stephen Colbert are just some of the new wave of talented folks who got their start in improv. As I wrote that, I realized that my version of "new wave" comedians are people in their forties and fifties. So allow Whistler's mother to continue.

Improvisational companies have become an invaluable training ground for so many successful comedians. Improv is as important a tool for an actor today as the methods of Stella Adler and Lee Strasberg were for actors beginning in the '50s. I have no doubt that the experience I received at Second City has had a lasting impact on my career. It taught me to stay present. There is no time for second-guessing when you improvise. You have to think on your feet, and if you are organically funny, it is the perfect vehicle in which to give voice to your comedic talent.

Which brings me, finally, again, to backstage at the Firehall Theatre and the creation of Edith Prickley.

The costumes on the dressing-room racks consisted of items we had either brought from our own homes or purchased cheaply at what was then known as Crippled Civilians, a used clothing store. Could there be a more politically incorrect name now? Crippled Civilians used to be on Jarvis Street, right around the corner from the Old Firehall theatre. It was a bargain basement of eclectic discarded outfits: oversized and shapeless wool overcoats, '50s party dresses, ratty bathrobes, ornately decorated and coloured sweaters—items that inspired the wackiest of characters in the wackiest of scenes. Also on the rack backstage was the '50s faux leopard jacket and hat that had belonged to Catherine O'Hara's mom.

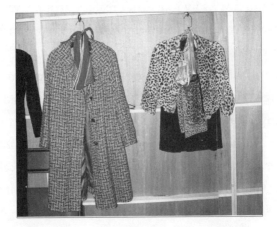

As the cast frantically brainstormed about the parent-teacher conference sketch, it was decided that Catherine would be the teacher and the rest of us would act as the obnoxious, unruly parents. We all started grabbing clothes and pinning up or slicking back our hair, and finding props to define our characters. Catherine combed her hair in a demure French twist and put on a skirt and cropped cardigan to complete the teacher look. The guys pulled glasses and suits and ties from the racks. I grabbed the leopard jacket and hat, put on a pair of rhinestone glasses I found on the costume-jewellery shelf, and smeared bright red lipstick on my mouth. We all then waited backstage to make our entrances one by one.

We improvised the scene on that cold night in 1977, and the audience loved it. In Second City, if an improvised scene went well, we continued to do it as an improv for a few months and, if was funny enough, it was then fully scripted and became one of the scenes in the next main show. Here's the scene:

"Teacher"

As the lights come up on the stage, Catherine, as the teacher, is writing on an imaginary chalkboard. Dave Thomas enters.

DAVE: Is this fourth grade?

CATHERINE: Yes, I'm Mrs. Meighan, the fourth-grade teacher. And you are . . . ?

DAVE: Bob Clarke.

CATHERINE: Oh, Tommy's father?

DAVE: Right.

CATHERINE: Thank you for coming to the meeting, Mr. Clarke.

DAVE: Is this some of their artwork?

CATHERINE: Yes, this is the children's artwork. That's Tommy's piece right there, the blank sheet of paper. I understand it meant something to him, so I put it up. Do you know what it is?

DAVE: It's a pictorial representation of the order of his mother's mind.

Eugene Levy enters.

CATHERINE: I'm Mrs. Meighen, and you are . . . ?

EUGENE: I'm Wayne's father.

CATHERINE: You're Mr. Klugie?

EUGENE: Yeah. How did you know?

CATHERINE: You said Wayne, Wayne Klugie.

EUGENE: Well, that's why you are the teacher!

CATHERINE: Thank you for coming to the meeting.

EUGENE: Well, I wanted to meet you 'cause Wayne has told me so much about you.

CATHERINE: Uh-oh.

EUGENE: Yes, he says you're the prettiest teacher in the whole wide world.

CATHERINE: He does?

EUGENE: Yes. And you know something? He was right! You are the prettiest teacher in the whole wide world.

CATHERINE: Oh, go on!

EUGENE: All right. (*He goes to exit.*)

CATHERINE: No! I didn't mean leave. Thank you for coming.

EUGENE: So! This is where the little critters do their learning, huh?

CATHERINE: Yes. This is where Wayne spends his days. Would you like to sit where he sits? He sits right here at the head of the class, right by me.

EUGENE: Oh wow! How about that! My Wayne right at the head of the class.

CATHERINE: Well, he sits there.

Andrea enters.

CATHERINE: I'm Mrs. Meighen, and you are . . . ?

ANDREA: I'm Sebastian's mother.

CATHERINE: Oh, Mrs. Prickley.

ANDREA: That's right, dear, Edith Prickley. Edith's the name, Sebastian's the game.

CATHERINE: It's nice to meet you.

ANDREA: Nice to meet you too, dear . . . You must be Slag Ass. That's what Sebastian says the kids all call you. No worries. You know how kids are . . . always saying it like it is. *Pahaaaaaa!!!!!*

CATHERINE: It is so important for parents to be involved in their children's schooling, and overseeing their homework is one of the best ways to do that. Don't you agree, Mrs. Prickley?

ANDREA: Absolutely, dear, I always help Sebastian with his homework. I say the family that plays together stays together. I do his homework, Sebastian pours the drinks! *Pahaaaaaa!!!!!* No, I'm kidding! I'd like to help Sebastian with his homework but I just don't have the time, dear. I've got my hands full with the hubby. Boy does he keep my hands full. *Pahaaaaaa!!!!!* (*Mimes juggling balls.*)

The scene continues as the parents become more unruly and the teacher becomes more frustrated. It culminates with Catherine yelling at the parents.

CATHERINE: I called you here because I thought we could have a dignified conversation about your children's problems, but now I realize that's impossible, *you* are your children's problems. And should never waste the teacher's time. Repeat after me, I should not waste the teacher's time.

ALL: I should not waste the teacher's time.

CATHERINE: Again.

ALL: I should not waste the teacher's time.

CATHERINE: Mrs. Prickley, a hundred times on the board.

ANDREA: *Me?*

CATHERINE: Yes! Now!

ANDREA: I should not waste the teacher's time . . .
Lights slowly fade out.

It was at that moment, on stage at the Old Firehall, that Edith Prickley was born. The posture, the voice, the intonation, the laugh, the volume, the name Edith all came together the minute I entered the scene and Catherine christened me Mrs. Prickley. When, while writing this book, I called Catherine to make sure I had the details correct, she reminded me that for a few weeks after that first time we performed "Teacher," she came up with a different name to introduce me, but the name Edith Prickley was so perfect, it stayed. And so did Mrs. Prickley's indefatigable laugh, *Pahaaaaaa!!!!!*

I have held on to Mrs. Prickley's leopard hat and jacket, and to her glasses, all these years. I still wear the costume when I perform the character at various benefits and in my one-woman shows. In 2008, Marty, Dave, Eugene, Joe, Catherine, and I performed "Teacher" at a Toronto fundraiser for the

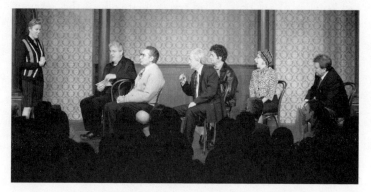

SCTV's Fiftieth Anniversary Benefit for the alumni fund.
From left to right: Catherine, Harold, Eugene, Marty, Joe, me, and Dave.

alumni of Second City. We were all on stage together. I looked around at my friends and was awestruck. We were still making each other laugh some thirty years later. I felt honoured and deeply moved to be there with them. During the show, and specifically in the scene "Teacher," we were kids again. No time had passed since 1977, when our careers were just beginning and the roots of *SCTV* were taking hold.

I have done everything in this house, including polishing eight butter knives that I have not used in twenty years, to avoid writing this chapter on *SCTV*. Everything. I have tried to make friends with the animals in my yard, which include a mongoose, two geese, two ducks, and two swans. No animal will have anything to do with me. They know I'm stalling, and they are not willing to enable me one minute more.

So, after I finish gathering and sorting every loose nail in my tool chest, I will open up my *SCTV* file, entitled "What Do You Think of This?," and try to write about those seven years that changed my life, that formed my career, that made it impossible to ever take direction from anyone on any subsequent TV show I did after *SCTV* went off the air in 1984. I will try to write about those glorious years with my talented friends, eight of the most gifted comic minds that have ever graced this planet: John Candy, Harold Ramis, Joe Flaherty, Martin Short, Dave Thomas, Eugene Levy, Rick

Moranis, Catherine O'Hara—and if I can accomplish just one-eighth of what we accomplished on TV with this book, I will be happy.

Patty Hearst was a nineteen-year-old socialite and heir to the William Randolph Hearst fortune when she was captured by the Symbionese Liberation Party, blindfolded, and allegedly locked in a closet for two months. When she was finally let out, she held up a bank and wrote letters to her family, calling them Communist pigs. Psychologists rushed to her defence and blamed her transformation on brainwashing, or the more fancy term, the Stockholm Syndrome. Her life was no longer about her; it was about the Symbionese Liberation Party and her fellow members.

Although I did not brandish a rifle and rob a bank, my life for my seven years with *SCTV* was not about me; it was about the nine of us. We were all blindfolded from the rest of the world and locked in a time capsule of collaboration and creative freedom. When you're in the zone, you're in your own time—in fact, you're beyond time. I was beyond time for seven years. Conjuring up the memories feels like a violation. I'm reluctant to revisit them. I don't want our experiences, which are sacred to me, to be exposed and misinterpreted. I want to protect the memories. Luckily because of the age I am, I can't remember specifics, but I can recall in broad strokes my devotion to my talented friends.

And yet, as I write this chapter, I feel lost, because there was nothing singular about those years. Everything about *SCTV* was the group. Where are my buddies, my fellow members? How I wish they were just down the hall, and I were back in our old writing offices in Toronto or Edmonton. I could meander my way into anyone's office, start brainstorming, pace around the room, laugh, collaborate, and laugh some more. By the end, something would have been written. And it would have been funny. How would we have measured that? From each other's laughter. Our written scenes would then be passed along a conveyor belt of creativity.

Wardrobe, headed by our darling Juul Haalmeyer and Trudy, his mom, designed elaborate costumes, sewing them from scratch; Makeup, led by the brilliant Bev Schectman and Christine Hart, researched and then drew and painted our faces like works of art; and Hair, designed by the incomparable Judi Cooper-Sealy, produced styles of stunning originality. All of these talented people collaborated closely with us and, in many cases, were responsible for creating the characters themselves. It wasn't until Bev suggested I paint my teeth a blinding white, Juul found a red plaid Scottish skirt and a starched white blouse with a plaid tie, and Judi created a mousy brown wig that I realized who Yolanda DeVilbis was.

She was the character on *SCTV* who recited the upcoming events in Melonville on her ten-minute weekly program,

Melonville Calendar. Upon seeing my white teeth, Catherine threw out a suggestion that timid Yolanda have a stutter as she recites the upcoming uninteresting events:

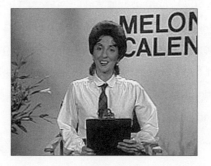

"This week at the Melonville Mixer, you can get three, free . . . free, three . . . three free fruit beverages. Orange . . . grape . . . and orange."

The writers, the actors, the crew, the director, the producers, the caterer, the janitor—anyone we asked, "What do you think of this?"—gave us their opinions. All of them were responsible for lifting our words off the page. Everyone supported each other and egged each other on. There was no one to squash our comedic impulses. We were kids in a playground, and comedy props and costumes were our toys. It was collaboration unlike anything I had ever experienced before or would after, and writing this chapter without the cast is as foreign to me as performing *SCTV* alone. And so I emailed my friends.

Dear cast and writers of *SCTV*:

I have been writing a book of essays for HarperCollins Canada for the last two years. I am near the end of the first draft and have yet to include *SCTV*. I am asking you if you would take a minute to email me what you think is worth remembering and what is worth forgetting about me during the show. I'm not asking you to do the writing; I just can't remember details, which begs the question, why am I writing a book? Which begs the bigger question, who in their right mind would read it?

Love and miss you all,

Andrea

Over the next week, I heard from Catherine:

Oh dear. I'm a woman in my fifties, but I'd be oh so happy to attempt to reminisce with you. It will be like Libby and Sue Bopper. On the bright side, I guess it means we're not that old. If we were, we'd have that excellent long-term memory. I look forward to laughing with you.

Mike Short, one of our writers and Marty's brother, emailed me that he had hundreds of stories—"What about the nine thousand times you showed the fellas your tits?" Bob Dolman, one of our talented writers and also my husband at the time of *SCTV*, wrote, "I remember something." And believe me, he did. I was so grateful to hear Bob's recollections, as he had a bird's-eye view of my time with *SCTV*.

He saw me in and out of the TV studio, in and out of our bed, and in and out of the maternity ward twice as I gave birth to our sons during those seven years.

As I was talking to each person, I realized we all remembered the smaller details differently but agreed on the larger picture: that we all trusted and looked out for each other.

I never heard back from Joe Flaherty but didn't expect to, he being the most eccentric person of the group. That's not to say that Joe won't appear just as I'm about to finish the book. And he'll undoubtedly have the most wisdom and the funniest take on our years together. But for now, he's probably using his frequent flyer miles to travel to countries all over the world, in no particular order and with no particular plan. He's always been a fanatic for accruing sky miles. Joe was the cheerleader and ringleader on *SCTV*, and his quick mind and sarcastic humour motivated me to write some of my favourite pieces. Without Joe, the *Evita* parody "Indira" or the *Annie* parody, starring a thirty-year-old

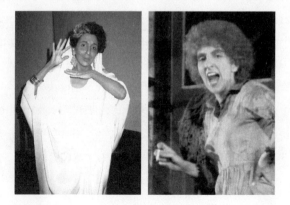

chain-smoking Andrea McArdle as nine-year-old Little Orphan Annie, would not have been written.

Joe had the ability to take something earnest and, with the slightest twist, turn it into something hysterically funny. He also had the gift of saying what everybody was thinking but was afraid to say. In a brainstorming meeting once, our producer, Nancy Geller, whom we all loved, pitched an idea, and the room went quiet. After a minute, Joe blurted out, "Uh, that's a really interesting and terrible idea, Nancy." Everybody burst into tears and laughter because we were all thinking that the idea was horrible, but who had the nerve to say so? It was Joe who had the courage.

During *SCTV*'s last year, on the US pay-cable station Cinemax, Catherine, who had left the show, came back to do our final episode. We had run out of money and yet had to deliver the eighteenth show. We were in the green room, and Catherine was improvising as Lola Heatherton, who had just got out of rehab. Joe laughed at everything Catherine did. "Look at her," he said. "She's just free. She can improvise and go off. It's like working with a genius." I said, "What about me, Joe?" He responded, "No, she's perfect. You, go learn your lines." And he walked out.

On second thought, I hope he doesn't respond to my email.

When I got in touch with Eugene, he wrote back:

My memory is worse than yours. Were you on the show?? Need
some time. Will get back ASAP.

Eugene

xo

His response was typical Eugene. That's how he wrote.
He would think and ponder and let an idea grow, and
when he was ready to write, he'd sit alone and meticu-
lously create a scene for the cast. But it was on his time-
table, because he had his own rhythm. He also could be
a little stubborn. Marty recalled my talking to Eugene
about a piece I had written and Eugene saying to me, "I
just wish I understood what the point of it was." He was
being sincere, and it never occurred to him that I might
be insulted. I leaned over with a pen in my hand and drew
an *X* on his pants over his penis and said, "That's so Deb
[Eugene's wife] can find it later." I loved making Eugene
laugh. Out of everyone I contacted, Eugene was the only
person to respond literally to the question I posed in my
email. After a week, he sent me what he referred to as his
"writing assignment" and said he hoped it was what I was
looking for. The following is his beautiful and funny recol-
lection of our time together:

If I were to guess what might have been the most forgettable
moments for you during our years doing *SCTV*, I would have to

say it was the table reads—those afternoons or, God forbid, those mornings when the writers and cast members would sit around a board table in a room with no windows and read the newly written scripts that were vying for placement in the next upcoming show. The reason the table reads were probably forgettable for you had nothing to do with how good or bad the scripts were or how good or bad the performance levels were, but pretty much had to do solely with the fact that every single writer and every single cast member smoked except for you. Come to think of it, I'm wrong. One of our writers, Dick Blasucci, also didn't smoke. But Dick's writing partner was Paul Flaherty, of the chain-smoking Flahertys, and Dick had spent so much time in a windowless office with Paul that he actually considered himself a smoker.

As each table read began, everyone would automatically reach for their deck of smokes and light up. By the time we got to the second script, the room was filled with the sweet Canadian scent of Rothmans, du Maurier, and Player's. At that point, you would reposition yourself to a chair in front of the open doorway. Fifteen people around the table and thirteen cigarettes lit—fifteen lit when you consider the Flahertys would oft times have two going at once. Your first ask to possibly not smoke during the process was always extremely polite, too polite for people to actually listen. Your second ask to put the cigs away was usually more forceful, as in *Hey, I'm really not kidding.* The response from your friends around the table? "Andrea, shut up!" By the time we were at the halfway point and you couldn't see people's faces through the clouds, you were a woman on a mission, citing health warnings, defining the meaning of "fairness," and protesting the God-given rights of the smoker. At that point, we would listen to your words, take a reflective moment or two, no wait, not two only one, one reflective moment, and give you the same response we would give you at the same point during every single table read: *You might be more comfortable in another room!*

Well, what can one say? It was the '70s. It was the '80s. It was a different time. Smoking was still cool. And non-smokers had no rights. Especially you. Looking back, it's a wonder you even showed up to those table reads. But maybe, just maybe, putting up with the ignorance and the arrogance was a small price to pay for the joy you must have felt hearing the laughs cascading through the smoke every time you got to read Edith Prickley! Maybe.

The first time I saw Marty Short was at the audition for the Canadian company of *Godspell*. He walked up on stage, at the old Masonic Temple in Toronto, and everyone fell in love with him. Entirely relaxed and uninhibited, he sang "My Funny Valentine" and sounded exactly like Frank Sinatra. He was adorable, with charm and charisma, and unlike anyone I had ever seen. The year was 1972. It was the beginning of all our careers. Marty met his future wife, Nancy Dolman, in *Godspell*, and they in turn introduced me to Nancy's brother, Bob, my future husband. We got married within two days of

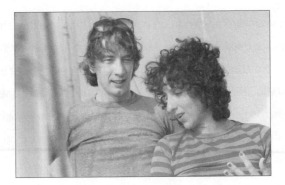

Marty and me, many moons ago

each other, honeymooned together, and have been in each other's lives for more than forty years.

I don't think it's possible to be objective about Marty. I worship the little fella. He is fearless and self-assured, and has taught me invaluable lessons in my life. His mantra about show business has always been *It's a business, take nothing personally*. Mine has been *It's a business, take everything personally*. He walks the talk. I have never met anyone, and especially in the business, less neurotic.

Here's an example of how he's been the voice of reason in my long career: during *every* rehearsal period, for *every* play I've ever been in, I will at one point call him and say, "Marty, in all seriousness, this time I've made a big mistake. I shouldn't have said yes to this part. I can't do it. How am I going to get out of it?" His response? "Very good. You've been saying the exact same thing since 1972. Look at your history. Have you ever failed? Goodbye."

We have worked so many times together only he would

be able to accurately recall the places and dates. He has an annoyingly precise memory. From *Godspell* in 1972 to Chrysler industrial shows, Second City, benefits for Second City, Marty's various television and animated TV shows, *SCTV*, commercials, Broadway readings, charity events, sitcoms, films, and skits in living rooms with friends and family across North America, we have developed a comedy shorthand that allows us to communicate and perform together, spontaneously and at the drop of a hat.

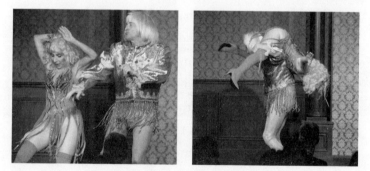

SCTV Fiftieth Anniversary Benefit, 2011

He and Nancy were second parents to Bob's and my sons, Jack and Joe. Their devotion and generosity to them over the years were limitless. And their beautiful children, Katherine, Oliver, and Henry, I love like my own. Marty is a great friend, and he's family. After all the years of hearing the same material, of watching and acting out the same stupid repetitive bits, I still laugh harder with Marty than I do with anyone else.

I'm hesitant to tell this next story because it makes me seem like a horrible person, but it's a great example of Marty's ability to be pragmatic and cut to the chase.

I was at a taping of a live TV reality show. I thought the host was mediocre. You know what? It's my book. She sucked. I was badmouthing her to the friends I was with throughout the show: "How the hell did she get this job? They don't make them less charismatic or less sincere." And I was saying this loudly. This was punctuated by me doing full-on impersonations of her blandness. My group laughed and laughed. When I got home that night, the producer of the reality show emailed me. He told me that the mother of the host was in the audience that night—in fact, sitting directly in front of me. She didn't turn around and ask me to stop. Instead, throughout the show, she texted her daughter *every word* that came out of my mouth. Not since the court-appointed stenographer in *Twelve Angry Men* has anyone transcribed that many words so quickly and accurately. The host herself wasn't a shy woman. She didn't receive the litany of insults and hide, as I would have. Instead, the producer informed me, she had waited in the parking lot to confront me. Thankfully, I had left before she made an appearance in Level Three, Section Bluebird. The producer wrote that he had given me free tickets and how dare I be so insensitive?

I was mortified and felt like a despicable human being. I called Marty immediately and told him the story.

First he laughed. Then he said, "So you got caught. That doesn't mean you're a bad person." And we moved on.

About the time that *SCTV* was ending, Dave Thomas said something to me that I never forgot: we might all have different experiences in our lives and go in different directions, and maybe not see each other often, but we would stay friends, and we'd be at each other's weddings—and at each other's funerals.

"Do you remember saying that, Dave?" I asked when I spoke to him on the phone. He was at home, in Los Angeles.

"Yes," said Dave. "Sure I remember. Because we had a pretty strong bond from the work. And those bonds were evident when somebody would come from the outside and interfere with the group. And then it was like arms were locked, and the strengths of each person became the strengths the person from the outside would have to deal with."

There was no outside world during *SCTV*. When we were filming, we spent seventeen hours a day in the studio. To add to the isolation, the studio itself was in the heart of Edmonton, a mere 2,160 miles from our homes in Toronto. We uprooted our families and lived in rented condos, which we basically never saw. Nor did we see any natural light, since the floor we worked on at ITV was completely underground. Nothing has been so dark and windowless since Dorothy Gale's storm shelter in *The Wizard of Oz*. When I say we worked seventeen hours a day, it wasn't just filming our own sketches. We were in each other's scenes, playing supporting parts or even working as extras, and when we weren't in the scenes, we would be on the set watching our fellow castmates in *their* scenes and giving notes, or laughing off camera, or telling them the best take, or suggesting another line. We had no audience at all. We and our crew were the audience. The only way we knew whether a sketch worked was if we made each other laugh. Thankfully, we weren't as critical as Dave Thomas's scathingly pithy theatre reporter, Bill Needle, who once reviewed Libby Wolfson's "I'm Taking My Own Head, Screwing It on Right, and No Guy's Gonna Tell Me That It Ain't" by summing it up with: "Libby Wolfson hit a new low by giving an unconvincing performance as herself."

Dave also came up with the sketch "Tex and Edna Boil's Organ Emporium" and selflessly backed up Edna on the organ as she relentlessly pitched the latest bargains and offerings.

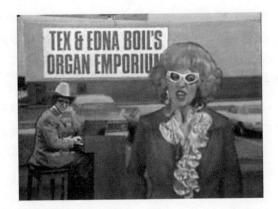

EDNA: Come on down to Tex and Edna Boil's Organ
Emporium, where me and my husband love you to
visit us. All this week we got rhythm aces for
$199.95, yes, we got rhythm aces and four and
a half miles of organs and pianos. So bring the
kids, bring the whole family. Right, Tex?
TEX: That's right, Edna.
EDNA: This week Tex will be cooking fresh farm
sausages, but keep those fingers off the merchan-
dise, the little piggies are greasy. So come on
down. It's Tex and Edna Boil's Organ Emporium.
That right, Tex?
TEX: That's right, Edna.

My angel, Catherine, Caterina, you darling girl. You gorgeous and talented writer, you brilliant performer, you kind
and giving soul. How I loved acting with Catherine, even
though we were so different as people, and so different in our
approach to the work. I would be waking up when she was
going to sleep. She loved improvising, and I loved a script
in my hand. She could go off by herself and come back with
the brilliant group scene "Night School High Q." (Who can
forget Margaret Meehan's plaintive "The Beatles?") I, however, needed to stand and pace and perform and hope that
the writers were taking every word down; the thought of
being alone and putting pen to paper was terrifying to me.
Catherine created some of my favourite sketches, including

"Way to Go, Woman!," which featured me as Mother Teresa and her as Lola Heatherton.

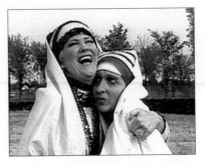

It juxtaposed a blonde narcissistic Vegas entertainer visiting the most saintly woman in the world. Instead of helping Mother Teresa tend to the poor, she forces her to pose for publicity photos.

We performed together as talk-show host Libby Wolfson and real estate agent and best friend Sue Bopper Simpson;

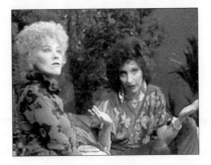

in "The Miracle Worker" as Helen Keller and Annie Sullivan (played by Edith Prickley); as the maid Mojo and her employer Mrs. MacKay in the soap opera "The Days of the Week"; as two older Jewish sisters in "How Nosy, the Short

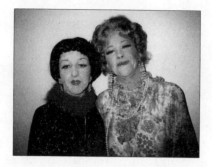

Haired Terrier Dog, Got His Name"; as Dutch van Dyke and her many unrequited crushes, all played by Catherine, and we sang as Anne Murray and Rita Coolidge in *SCTV*'s Anne Murray special.

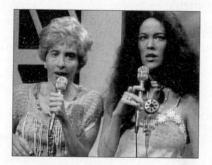

The list is endless.

Over the years, the one sketch people ask me about consistently is one I did with Catherine, "English for Beginners." They ask me how it was created, and here and now, I want to give credit where credit is due. The sketch was originated

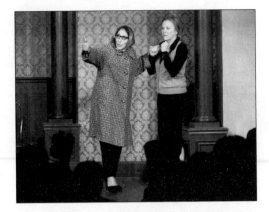

by Dan Aykroyd and Valri Bromfield on stage at Toronto's Second City. Dan played the student; Valri, the teacher. We filmed the sketch for *SCTV* with Catherine as the teacher, now named Lucille Hitzger, and me as the student, a woman of nondescript ethnicity, wearing a winter overcoat and babushka, named Perini Scleroso. Lucille tries desperately to teach Perini common English phrases like "Can you direct me to the hotel?" and Perini tries her best but can only sound out "Can oo eetrac me tu na lo to?" As Lucille gets more and more frustrated, she keeps repeating, "Can you direct me to the hotel?" and Perini keeps repeating "Can oo eetrac me tu na lo to?" until Lucille breaks down and blurts out, "Can oo eetrac me tu na lo to?" There is silence. Perini stares at her for a moment, takes her hand, and says, "Sure, honey. You just go down two blocks. You can't miss it."

I like to think that Catherine and I were a good team, we two women who looked out for each other and complemented each other's talent. We had such creative freedom on *SCTV*. Where else could we have filmed an entire twenty-minute segment focusing on two middle-aged marginally talented women who write what they think is a groundbreaking feminist musical manifesto, "I'm Taking My Own Head, Screwing It on Right, and No Guy's Gonna Tell Me That It Ain't"?

The opening number lyrics included:

```
Menopause, stretch marks, sagging skin
Kinda like the shape that we're all in!
This play is by women, for women, full
   of women and women thoughts!
[As we flashed our legs.] But men don't
   go away, you're welcome to stay . . .
   that's if you're man enough . . . to
   love . . . women!
```

As her career after *SCTV* attests, Catherine will not take a job if it does not have meaning to her. She's discerning and particular and picky, whereas I come from the summer stock mentality—give me a set and a costume and some funny glasses, throw me on stage, and I'll "put on a show!" It was an honour to work with Catherine, and I continue to be an unwavering fan of hers. It is my dream to one day perform with her in a play on Broadway and have the opportunity to create another dynamic duo, this time on stage. And you can bet I'll be working my ass off just to keep up with the likes of her.

* * *

I'm grateful for the time Rick Moranis and I had together. Rick was an exceptional writer, a visionary. He created the character Gerry Todd, a VJ . . . *years* before there were VJs. In those early days, Rick would come to the studio with legal pads filled with ideas. He was prolific and had a great sense of television. He knew how to use the camera to make a joke land—how to get a laugh by setting a shot a different way. He was way ahead of his time. And I loved performing and writing the Libby Wolfson scenes when he'd join me as another character. Like Dave Thomas, he would let me shine in a sketch where he didn't have that many lines. He understood and loved the neuroses of Libby Wolfson, a self-centred woman who for some reason had her own

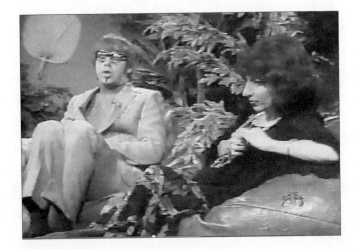

talk show, on which she consistently turned the conversation back to herself and her many insecurities. So many of the characters we played on *SCTV* were based on people we knew. I created Libby Wolfson and her talk show *You!* from watching Micki Moore, who had her own TV show on CityTV in Toronto during the '80s. Libby's set didn't have chairs. Instead, it was a platform with tons of pillows that she and her guests had to awkwardly sit on.

One of Libby Wolfson's many neuroses was her obsession with smells. Her talk show always began something like this:

```
Music: "You Are So Beautiful."
```

Libby sits uncomfortably on the many pillows. She speaks directly to the camera.
LIBBY: Is there a cat in here? It's that male spray thing I don't like the smell of. What is it, onions? (*She smells her fingers.*) Wait, no, I'm sorry. It's tabbouleh, serves me right for eating with my fingers.

Rick joined me a few times on the show as the in-house psychiatrist, Sol Rubin.

LIBBY: Dr. Sol Rubin is here to talk about a problem that affects so many women today . . . women's problems.

Rick begins to give an overview of women's issues in the context of modern-day feminism as Libby is distracted, nervously fixing her hair and makeup and smelling her underarms.

She then asks him, "What about weight? You see a lot of women who are fat, right?"

He is perplexed by the question but responds in a professional manner.

DR. SOL RUBIN: Well, I see a lot of women who have compulsive issues. Some women are overweight and some are anorexic.

LIBBY: (Leans forward.) You know what? I'd kill to be anorexic for one week, can I tell you that? (He doesn't respond.) Continue.

(He begins a sentence and Libby yet again cuts him off.) Why can I not stop eating? You're a doctor, you should know. If there was a roll there, I'd eat it. Is that not sick?

He tries to reposition himself on the pillows and before he answers, the theme music comes up, prompting Libby to close the show. But she praises him for how enlightening it's been to have him as a guest.

We knew those characters inside out, and improvising their dialogue was, dare I say, second nature for us. It was also delirious fun working together with Rick as Libby's boyfriend, businessman Lenny Schectman.

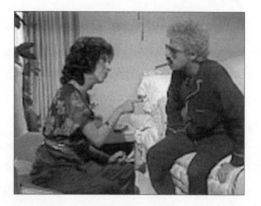

One of my favourite moments in the sketch is a scene with Libby and Lenny at home. Libby is working on "I'm Taking My Own Head, Screwing It on Right, and No Guy's Gonna Tell Me That It Ain't." Lenny is angry with her for spending so much time on her upcoming show. They are in the middle of an argument when Libby suddenly says to Lenny, "Go like this," gesturing to him to let her smell his breath. He breathes out. "Did you have hot dogs for dinner?" she asks. "Yes," says Lenny. "Do you have any more?" Libby asks. He tells her there are some in the freezer. They then continue their argument.

We did numerous sketches together, but the Libby scenes with Rick will always be among my favourites.

The late great Harold Ramis, way before he wrote *Caddyshack* and wrote and starred in *Ghostbusters*, was *SCTV*'s head writer for a brief time as we were launching the show. When I think of him, I picture him doing crossword puzzles. It was his way to relax. In between takes, he'd pull out a puzzle and fill in the blanks with the speed of someone playing tic-tac-toe. I was always slightly intimidated by Harold's intelligence. I looked up to him. When he moved on to write and perform in movies, it was a great loss for *SCTV*. He brought profound humanity to every piece he wrote and acted in, and I loved him. We all did.

He wrote for me two of my favourite *SCTV* sketches: a commercial for Connie Francis, who was a big star in the '50s. I was a fan of her film *Where the Boys Are*, and thanks to her Italian heritage, I could look like her convincingly enough to impersonate her. I had noticed that her songs always sounded sad, so Harold wrote a K-tel record ad for Connie, whom we called Connie Franklin. Connie stands alone on a stage with a bright spotlight on her as she sings despondently:

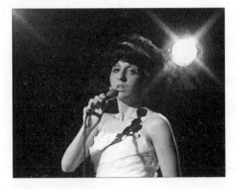

```
I'm losing my hearing,
I've lost sight in one eye.
I'm sorry I can't hear you,
Did you really say goodbye?
```

ANNOUNCER: Yes, Connie Franklin, the most depressing singer of her generation, will really bring
you down with twenty of her most depressing hits.

We then hear Connie continuing, "Stop slapping my face
now."

Harold also co-wrote "Sex Talk with Dr. Cheryl Kinsey"
with me. Dr. Kinsey was an incredibly uptight woman who
had a nervous tic whenever anything sexual was mentioned.

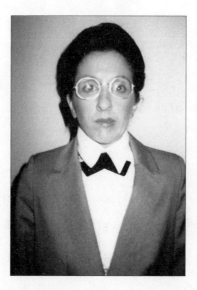

DR. KINSEY: Welcome ladies to today's seminar, Sex,
Sex, and More Sex . . . Today I want to talk to you
about one of the most common sexual dysfunctions
in women today. The inability to fake orgasms.
Recent studies show that nearly 60 percent of all

women are capable of at least one fake orgasm, and nearly 20 percent of these women report multiple fake orgasms. That leaves 40 percent, four out of ten women, who are unable to convincingly fake an orgasm. If you are one of these women, may I suggest the following exercise. Please repeat after me, these helpful passionate phrases: (*With no affect, yet involuntary physical twitching.*) "Don't stop, lover, please . . . don't stop." "Oh, you're good, you're so good." And "Stuff me like a mushroom, big boy."

Fortunately, in a recent study, it was shown that nine out of ten males will believe anything, especially if it confirms their virility, so don't be afraid to pretend you're aroused by your partner.

I was so thrilled that Harold cast me in his film *Club Paradise*, and the shower scene he wrote for me remains one of the funniest scenes I've ever had the great pleasure to do.

Johnny LaRue, John Candy, Johnny Toronto, Johnny Chicago. Anywhere John Candy went, he was worshipped and adored. The police, the queen of England, the janitor. It didn't matter who you were or the status you had, John treated everyone the same. He was exactly as you would like to think he was. He was actually *that* guy. I'd see him with fans who had come up to him on the street and started acting out their favourite scenes with him, and he'd go along with anything.

John was the first person I knew who had an entourage. There were always people in his dressing room, from all walks of life. It's been twenty years since John died, but I'm still stopped by people, especially working-class guys, who ask me about *SCTV* and say how sad it is that John is no longer with us. Even those hulking guys let their guard down as tears fill their eyes, their grief over the death of John Candy, a man they never knew, overwhelming them.

Everything John did was big. Bob told me about the time he was writing a sketch with John. It was ten pages long. Bob said, "John, we've got to cut it down." "You're right, Bob," said John, "I'll take it home and work on it this weekend."

"He came back Monday," Bob told me, "and said he rewrote it—and it was now twenty pages long."

Bob once went out to write with John on his farm, but they got no work done because John had so many things going on. He was having a radar dish installed, and gardeners building a river. He showed Bob a barn that housed every car he'd ever owned. He wasn't able to give anything away.

What John did share was his deep vulnerability and authenticity. There wasn't a cynical bone in his body. I would have loved to see where his career would have taken him. He was not only capable of making you laugh, he could also make you cry, which you'd know if you saw *Trains, Planes and Automobiles*. He was a singular actor and a heartbreaking clown, and the world still mourns his loss.

My favourite scene with John Candy: In August 1981, the accomplished actress Lynn Redgrave sued Universal Television, claiming she had been fired from *House Calls,* a sitcom in which she played a nurse. She had been told she could not breastfeed her baby during breaks in shooting. I had just given birth to my first son, Jack, in July of that year. We took the incident and turned it into a promo sketch called "Wet Nurse." It begins in a hospital waiting room with me dressed as a nurse and my back to the camera. Joe Flaherty, as the doctor, is talking to me with overly dramatic urgency:

"Nurse, there's a total power failure in the cafeteria. Every patient in this hospital is starving. You are the only one that can help us. We are counting on you."

I turn to face camera, and viewers can see for the first time my ginormous boobs, a foot in diameter. "Yes, doctor," I say as I run toward camera, my boobs filling the screen.

We then hear the announcer, voiced by Rick Moranis:

"Coming to *SCTV* this fall, *Wet Nurse*, starring Lynn Redgrave, a woman dedicated to the sustenance and nurturing of all mankind."

The scene cuts to me with a little baby, who in real life was my two-month-old son, Jack. He is perilously balanced on my shoulder. My gigantic boobs keep him suspended as I walk around the room. I put him on my lap and begin to unbutton my shirt to breastfeed him. There's a time lapse and the baby is now John Candy. He is on my lap, in the same position, dressed identically to my real baby, and I'm burping him. The camera pans down to my boobs, which are now flat and deflated as I rock all three hundred pounds of Baby John. He coos and smiles gleefully as he is bounced up and down.

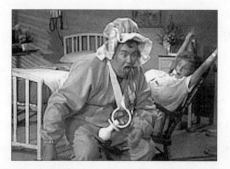

I am not sure you could show that sketch today on prime time anywhere because women with big breasts would feel discriminated against. Breastfeeding advocates would think

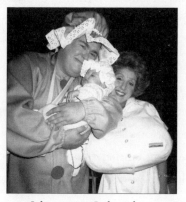

John, my son Jack, and me

we were admonishing them, not to mention the child abuse charges brought against me for recklessly balancing my son on my shoulder.

We had so much social and creative freedom on *SCTV*. The world wasn't picky about being politically correct, and we never thought a lot about it because we were isolated from the press, and the media, and we were having so much damn fun. Lynn Redgrave, like so many actors I had impersonated, became a friend, and she was delighted to have been portrayed so comically. When I was acting in the film *Stepping Out* with Liza Minnelli, I was terrified that she had seen my impersonation of her, whom we called Lorna Minnelli. Over the three months we worked together, she never mentioned seeing it—until our last day, when she took me aside and said, "I've seen you do me. You're *terrific*."

Brenda Vaccaro, Linda Lavin, Bernadette Peters, Anne Murray, Andrea McArdle, Barbra Streisand. Not one of these women, all of whom I have impersonated and was later introduced to, ever confided in me that they were upset or insulted by my impersonations of them.

I'm sorry I never met Mother Teresa because I know she would have had the utmost forgiveness of my portrayal of her in Lola Heatherton's show. We realized while doing *SCTV* that people love being impersonated—it is the highest form of flattery. At least no one told us differently. We made it a

The Juul Haalmeyer, Bev Schectman, and Judi Cooper-Sealy Hall of Fame

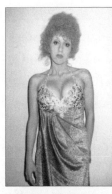

Bernadette Peters

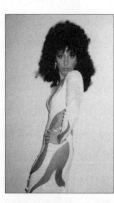

Cher

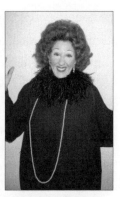

Ethel Merman

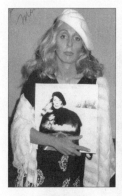

Joni Mitchell

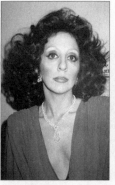

Sophia Loren

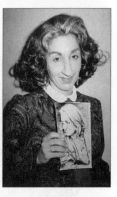

Betty Friedan

point never to be mean-spirited. Our comedy was not cynical. Overall, we had a reverence for what we were making fun
of. One of my favourite sketches was "Farm Film Celebrity
Blow-Up," starring John Candy and Joe Flaherty. It was a perfect vehicle in which to impersonate famous actors—or let's
be honest, people we could look like.

In this sketch, celebrities were blown up because of
something irritating they did or were known for, and it
never failed to make me laugh. It sounds cruel now, the act
of blowing someone up, but when you watch the sketch,
you see innocence and glee and mischievousness in John's
and Joe's eyes, not cruelty, and because of the fun they are
having, the audience is having fun too.

Eugene Levy did a spot-on impression of Neil Sedaka. He
sounded and looked exactly like him. As he sits behind the
piano, Joe and John question him about his high voice.

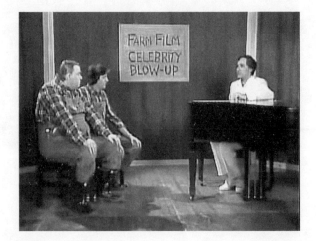

Eugene, as Neil, lets us know that he knows he's going to be blown up. And he's excited about it, just as long as John and Joe stop making fun of his high voice. He continues to sing, and when he is asked to sing even higher and does so willingly, he is blown up in a puff of smoke.

It is hysterical, in the same tradition as the "Nairobi Trio," the unforgettable Ernie Kovacs sketch from the '50s. Four people dressed in gorilla suits perform the same musical piece week after week. Despite the predictability of the routine, the impeccable timing of the actors and their physical comedy always made me laugh. Our scenes worked because we exaggerated an element of truth about the celebrities we were impersonating.

Most actors will tell you that the best part of a job is getting it—and then it's downhill from there. In the theatre, the best part for me is the rehearsal process. Because you're exploring, figuring things out, discovering things, changing things, not being judged. *SCTV*, for its seven years, was a rehearsal. Every day was a discovery. We were writing new scenes all the time. We didn't have a formula. We created a fictional TV station, SCTV, and we had freedom to program it any way we wanted. We wrote film parodies, news broadcasts, commercials, morning shows, late-night shows, game shows, talk shows, and entire shows built around musical acts who were guest stars. Everyone brought his or her personal experiences and unique talents to the writing rooms, and everyone had his or her own particular writing style.

We didn't worry whether people would like what we wrote or performed. In fact, we never thought much about the audience. We never even thought anyone was watching. We were isolated in studios in Toronto and in Edmonton without any live audience. There wasn't the Internet, Twitter, Facebook, iPhones with cameras, paparazzi, and so on. No distractions and no feedback. We were in a creative bubble. We were never thinking, *What can this show lead to? What will it get us?* When you have that toxic expectation, it's impossible to do your best work.

In 2008, *SCTV* was honoured at the Comedy Festival in Aspen, Colorado. My castmates and I sat on a panel on stage, in front of a big screen on which scenes from *SCTV* were projected. Conan O'Brien moderated and conducted interviews with us.

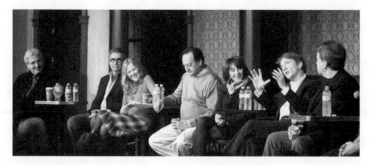

A huge audience had gathered. We couldn't believe the laughter from the audience. It's not that all the scenes were amazingly funny. It's just that we had been on our own, on stages in Toronto and Edmonton, for seven years, and we'd never heard live laughs. We had only heard laughs from one another.

When I started writing this chapter, I felt a huge responsibility. I didn't know how to tell this story. It was not up to me to represent my friends, and thirty years later, we are still friends. It was up to them to tell their story. But how do you extricate yourself from your family? We grew up together. We were just starting out in our lives and careers when we met. We began in the '70s, when comedy was as hip as rock 'n' roll, when comedians were on the front page of *Rolling Stone*. By the '80s, we were going our separate ways. Some of us were married or were about to be married. Our family grew. We had children and then more children, and our careers went in different directions. We remain very close today. We are at each other's theatre and film openings, birthday parties, kids' weddings, holidays, summer cottages, and, tragically in a few instances, as Dave Thomas poignantly pointed out, each other's funerals.

People ask us all the time if there will be a reunion. None of us has any interest in trying to recreate those years, or to show up looking older and decrepit and then have that become the focus—how we aged, rather than how we made people laugh. Today, you can buy the seven seasons of *SCTV* collected on DVD. That's enough of a reunion for us. We see our kids laughing at the same things that made us laugh thirty years ago, and it's both heartwarming and validating that our comedy may just be timeless.

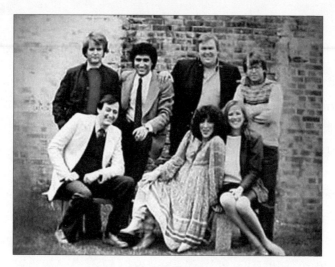

Cast of *SCTV*, 1981

Everything Must Go

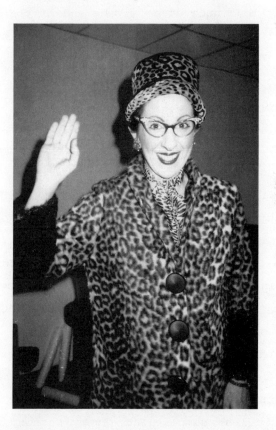

EDITH PRICKLEY: Well, there you go, folks. Ms. Martin ended that *SCTV* chapter on a whimsical note, which seems to be her gushingly sentimental style, but not mine! When I reminisce, there's nothing sentimental about it. I know how to be concise.

Let me tell you about the time I met Mr. Prickley. I saw him in the touring company of *Hair*. He was playing the role of Woof. He did that famous nude scene at the end of the first act, I took one look at him, and that's what I said, "*Woof*." He proposed to me that night. What he proposed, I'm not prepared to tell you, but it involved three girls from the show, a trapeze, and a Shetland pony. That was my introduction to show business. Unfortunately, that's not what the vice squad called it. *Pahaaaaaa!!!!!*

And that's enough about the past, mine and Andrea's. It's time to move forward. I'm on the yes train, baby. Pure and simple. As my old lover, the Dalai Lama, once said to me on a cold morning in a hut in Tibet when he broke his vows and wouldn't get his hands out of my pants, "Choose to be optimistic. It feels better." I don't know what the hell he was talking about, but as soon as I said yes, I felt better. Luckily he got back on track and now he's saving the world. My life is less complicated. Every morning, with Mr. Prickley by my side, I give thanks. I get down on my knees, Mr. Prickley's gorgeous manly parts in full view, and *woof*, do I give thanks.

Pahaaaaaa!!!!! I just keep going, moving forward, and so must you. Stay on that yes train, folks, until the big man upstairs says "Knock it off." Yes, eventually everything must go, including this godforsaken book. So put your hands together and let's bring this baby home!

Rapper L'il Edith P.

What am I supposed to do? Shrivel up and
   cry now?
Menopause and then applause and "Thank
   you, can I die now?"
What, I'm pushin' sixty? So, suddenly I'm
   sickly?
Hey, suck this Dixie cup, I am Edith
   Prickley!

All my life, I have barrelled through
   every stoplight
So sorry, baby starlets, I don't wanna
   leave the spotlight
Give me the love, give me the stage,
   give me the laughter
Give me the thirty-two-ounce margarita
   after

I can garden, I can bake
I can shimmy, I can shake
You can stay on golden pond,
I'm skinny dipping in this lake

I'm Prickley and I'm proud
Prickly and I'm loud
I'm wearing leopard print
So you can pick me in a crowd

Give me the energy to live and never
  settle
Put the pedal to the metal from the
  ghetto to the shtetl
Fuck Gepetto, I'm pulling my own string
'Cause I got my own song to sing
I told you everything must . . . *WHAT?*
Everything must . . . *WHAT?*
Everything must GO!

Epilogue

A couple of years ago, I was spending the afternoon at the Whitney Museum in New York, taking in all the wondrous art of Edward Hopper. I saw out of the corner of my eye a woman staring at me and then avert her gaze. *Oh boy,* I thought. *Can't a celebrity get some downtime without being bothered by her fans? Is there always paparazzi lurking about? Don't I deserve a little privacy? Am I going to have to pull an Alec Baldwin and punch her out?* At that moment, I felt a tap on my shoulder. It was the woman. She spoke quietly and hesitantly. "Excuse me," she said, "I don't mean to bother you. But . . . are you Cher's mother?"

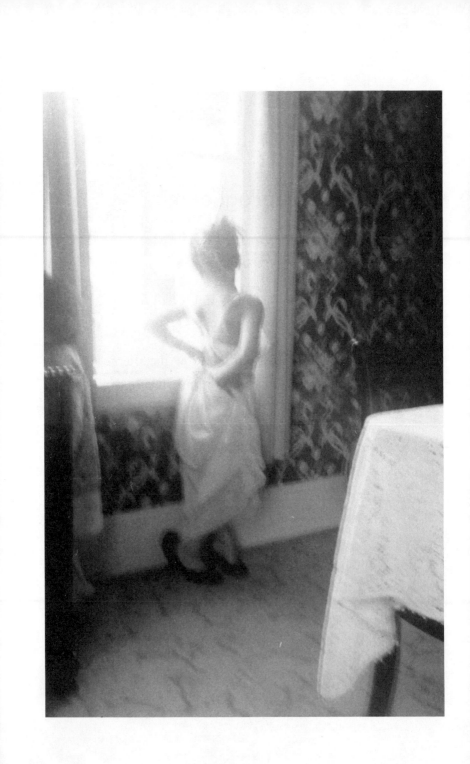

Acknowledgements

Books are hard to write, but easier if you have the following people in your corner:

Seth Rudetsky, James Wesley, Matt Roberts, David Feldman, Nathan Lane, Sam Wasson, Linda Wallem, Bruce Villanch, Walter Bobbie, Dani Klein Modisett, Marc Shaiman, Scott Wittman, Sean Hayes, and Mel Brooks. THANK YOU.

Thank you to Andrew Alexander and Second City, Ivan Reitman, Barry Weissler, Stephan Schwartz, and Lin-Manuel Miranda for allowing me to reproduce material.

To Paul Trusciani, for your generosity and loving reminiscences of my father. To my sister, Marcie, my brother, Peter, my cousin Stephanie Stearns, my sons, Jack and Joe Dolman, for your unconditional love. To my extended Armenian family, who gave me my roots, and to my hairdresser, Pascal, who restored them to their natural colour.

To Mel Morgan, for your patience and computer savvy.

To Deb Monk, my dear friend and life coach.

To Judi Cooper-Sealy and Bev Schectman, for your artistry and your Poloroids.

Thank you Bob Dolman, Catherine O'Hara, Martin Short, Mike Short, Eugene Levy, Dave Thomas, and Dick Blasucci for answering my emails, and reigniting my memory of our *SCTV* years together.

To Perry Zimel, my manager, for walking me into the HarperCollins boardroom, and to Jim Gifford, my editor, who greeted me at the door and stayed by my side. THANK YOU all from the bottom of my heart. I seriously could not have written this book without you.

Credits

A ll photographs courtesy the author, except as follows: p. 17 "KIT KAT® is a registered trademark of Société des Produits Nestlé S.A., Vevey, Switzerland, used with permission; p. 141 used with permission; p. 142 courtesy the Johnny Carson Estate, used with permission; p. 273 (Golde) courtesy Carol Rosegg, used with permission; p. 273 (Frau Blucher), photograph © Paul Kolnik, used with permission; pp. 275 and 276 (Aunt Voula) photography by Sophie Giraud, courtesy of Gold Circle Films, used with permission; p. 279 courtesy Dan Goldberg and Ivan Reitman, used with permission; p. 291 courtesy Barry Weissler, used with permission; pp. 19, 280, 281, 293, 300, 305, 309, 311, 316, 317, 320, 322–23, 324, 326, 329–31, 335, 337–38, 340, 342–43 courtesy The Second City Entertainment, Inc. and Fireworks Entertainment. Inc., used with permission.